BRITAIN'S BEST POLITICAL CARTOONS 2024

Dr Tim Benson is Britain's leading authority on political cartoons. He runs the Political Cartoon Gallery and Café which is located near the River Thames in Putney. He has produced numerous books on the history of cartoons, including *David Low Censored*, *Giles's War*, *Low and the Dictators*, *The Cartoon Century: Modern Britain through the Eyes of Its Cartoonists*, *Drawing the Curtain: The Cold War in Cartoons*, *Over the Top: A Cartoon History of Australia at War*, *How to be British: A Cartoon Celebration*, *Churchill: A Life in Cartoons* and *Drawn to the Promised Land: A Cartoon History of Britain, Palestine and the Jews: 1917–1949*.

BRITAIN'S BEST POLITICAL CARTOONS 2024

Edited by Tim Benson

HUTCHINSON
HEINEMANN

1 3 5 7 9 10 8 6 4 2

Hutchinson Heinemann
Penguin Random House
One Embassy Gardens
8 Viaduct Gardens
London SW11 7BW

Hutchinson Heinemann is part of the Penguin
Random House group of companies whose addresses
can be found at global.penguinrandomhouse.com

First published in the UK by Hutchinson Heinemann in 2024

www.penguin.co.uk

A CIP catalogue record for this book is available from the British Library

ISBN 9781529154733

Typeset in 11/15.5pt Amasis MT Light by Jouve (UK), Milton Keynes
Printed and bound in Italy by L.E.G.O. S.p.A.

The authorised representative in the EEA is Penguin Random House Ireland,
Morrison Chambers, 32 Nassau Street, Dublin D02 YH68

Penguin Random House is committed to a sustainable future
for our business, our readers and our planet. This book is made
from Forest Stewardship Council® certified paper.

INTRODUCTION

A recent advertisement for a cartoonist workshop at the *Guardian* includes the following couple of sentences:

> If you are part of an under-represented group through your race, gender, disability, age, sexual orientation or religion, or come from a socially or economically disadvantaged background, we invite you to apply. You'll learn what it takes to be a *Guardian* cartoonist: everything from the kind of brief you're given, to the generation of ideas, to completing your artwork within tight time constraints.

This appeal to as diverse a range of candidates as possible both reflects contemporary concerns and attitudes and, implicitly, sheds a certain light on the rather more uniform nature of cartooning and cartoonists that has, essentially, prevailed right up to the present day. The fact is that for 250 years or so cartooning has tended to be the preserve of a particular, quite narrow section of society: largely middle class, predominantly white, male and British – from Gillray, Tenniel, Partridge, Strube and Low to Illingworth, Cummings, Trog, Garland, Bell and Brookes. True, the great David Low was a New Zealander, who worked for a while in Australia, but his background scarcely constituted an obstacle when it came to taking up a post at the London *Star*.

Such exceptions as there have been proved relatively few and far between, at least until the 1930s and 1940s when national newspapers employed a number of (mostly emigré) Jewish cartoonists for the first time in Fleet Street's history: Victor Weisz (born in Berlin), Philip Zec (the son of a tailor from Odessa), Ralph Sallon (from Poland) and Stephen Roth (from Czechoslovakia). As late as the 1960s, the only person of colour to work as a full-time cartoonist in the UK was the Indian-born Attupurathu Abraham – better known as Abu – who was employed by the *Guardian*. The first female cartoonist whose work figured regularly in the national press was Margaret Belsky, who worked for the *Daily Herald* in the 1950s, although she was a pocket cartoonist and would sign her cartoons only with her surname to obscure her gender. It's only in the last ten years that female political cartoonists (one of the most talented being Nicola Jennings, whose work features on the cover of this volume) have become regular contributors to national newspapers – most frequently the *Guardian*. A rare example of a disabled cartoonist is Carl Giles, who worked for the *Daily Express* from the 1940s to the 1990s, despite having lost his sight in one eye and hearing from one ear following a motorcycle accident when he was 19.

This historical imbalance has, according to the *Daily Telegraph*, prompted London's Cartoon Museum in 2020 to consider remedial action:

> Officials at the Cartoon Museum are preparing to strip back displays of some of Britain's best known satirists because the galleries are over-represented by 'white cisgender men'. Curators at the London institution say they are 'interrogating' its collection of 6,000 cartoons and comic artwork to address an 'inherent bias' favouring white cartoonists . . . Joe Sullivan, the museum director, said: 'From our perspective, our collection – like many museums – is overrepresented with works by white cisgender men, which of course includes essential and significant works from artists such as H. M. Bateman, James Gillray, William Hogarth. From my point of view, and the Cartoon Museum, we are definitely moving towards displaying less Hogarths and more modern and diverse work.'

The wisdom of such an intention is, in my view, highly questionable. As L. P. Hartley wrote in 1953, 'The past is a foreign country: they do things differently there.' You can't rewrite history. The fact that great cartoonists of the past tended to share a certain background doesn't, in my view, make them any less worthy of being displayed or celebrated. Nor is it possible to display a historical archive of what – however unfairly – doesn't exist. Removing work by 'cisgender men' would in effect cancel proven world-class cartoonists and misrepresent the cartooning world of earlier generations.

The appeal by the *Guardian* for cartoonists from as wide a background as possible is worthy, but there are a few problems with it. It doesn't mention that cartooning is an insecure and unreliable career and that there are scarcely half a dozen full-time positions in the national press. Nor does it acknowledge that those

Patrick Blower's cartoon was featured in the *Daily Telegraph* on 29 January 2024 after it was reported that the Royal Navy was redeploying sailors as diversity and inclusion officers.

cartoonists currently in post tend to see it as a vocation and so rarely retire, with the result that even just one of those full-time positions rarely comes up. At 88, Mac still draws for the *Mail on Sunday*. Peter Brookes at *The Times* is a spring chicken by comparison, but he is nevertheless 81 years old. Andy Davey, cartoonist for the *Daily Telegraph*, outlines the issue as follows:

> Newspapers hang on to cartoonists who tend to carry on until they can no longer hold a quill, so there is a legacy of paleness, maleness and staleness. I'm not saying that

Old White Men are a bad thing (speaking as one), just that there are so few perches for cartoonists of any stripe. In addition to that, newspapers are read by fewer and fewer people, so young budding satirists of diverse backgrounds might see nothing attractive about working in a dying medium.

Above all, the *Guardian* advertisement doesn't talk about the one factor that should surely determine whether or not someone should consider a cartooning career: talent. Cartooning should be open to everyone, and I mean everyone. That, of course, is a given. However, the most important thing is that every wannabe must possess the talent to compete with the very best in the industry. In the past, the cream has always risen to the top – as the cartoonists at *The Times*, for example, have constantly demonstrated. And that's exactly as it should be. In my view, ability should be the sole consideration. 'I can say that I have never been given a job based on my gender, colour, age or anything else that can be confidently determined by meeting me in person,' says the *Sun*'s Steve Bright. 'The vast majority of my clients/employers over the years never met me before I started working for them, and since the advent of email have never spoken to me. My pen name, Brighty, derives from my surname and gives nothing away, but anyone who thinks it reflects upon my intellect would be sorely disappointed. I am hired by the quality of my work only, as I suspect the vast majority of cartoonists are. Which is exactly as it should be.' Just as, in my view, the Cartoon Museum should focus on the best of the past, so the *Guardian* should focus on finding the best for the future.

* * *

Those two sentences in the *Guardian* advertisement and the Telegraph piece about the Cartoon Museum are likely to evoke a one-word response from some: 'woke'. It's a term that has been floating around for a while – one that arose among the Black community in the United States to describe someone who is educated about social injustice or, as the *Guardian*'s Nicola Jennings puts it, is 'aware of social inequality' or, alternatively, in Andy Davey's words, someone who is keen to see the 'shedding of old, long-held prejudices; the prejudices of the powerful towards the powerless'. And it's a word that, for those on the right, has become something of a pejorative term. For them it implies at best empty 'virtue signalling', at worst the unfair promotion of one set of causes and interests over another. In November 2023 Prime Minister Rishi Sunak appointed Esther McVey minister responsible for the government's 'anti-woke' agenda, which was characterised and defended by her husband as being in part a counterattack on the 'huge amount of taxpayers money wasted on this equality, diversity and inclusion thing'.

The cartoonist known as 'Dormouse' imagines what Esther McVey's uniform might be as the new minister for the 'anti-woke' agenda. This image was featured in *North West Bylines* in November 2023.

Anti-wokeness has become something of a clarion call for certain national newspapers, notably the *Telegraph*. 'It's something that exercises the *Daily Telegraph* and that is basically it,' says Steve Bell. 'They have a whole raft of psychopaths who write columns on the subject in order to appease their readers.' Andy Davey, who works for the newspaper in question, acknowledges that 'papers that publish my work are like the majority of the UK media right-wing, which means their natural position will mostly be "anti-woke"'.

Like all value-laden terms that evade precise definition, 'wokeness' is very much in the eye of the beholder. One person's wokery is another's good manners. Christian Adams suggests that it has become such an obsession with the right-wing press that it no longer really has any meaning at all. The *Daily Mail* for one, he suggests, 'is using it to describe the most random of things. Roads, animals, the weather.' Steve Bright argues that 'Woke has no easy definition these days. People use the term to suit their own agendas, and what was once a word that stood for social and political enlightenment and awareness (something we should all aspire to, I think) has been weaponised by those who make demands that go well beyond an understanding of the feelings of others, and in turn "woke" has become a pejorative by those who fear it infringes on their values. Today's woke is a bastardisation of its original meaning, and the nemesis of its own etymology.' At its worst, according to Andy Davey, 'it can be hijacked by angry people who want to provoke a reaction by

being more and more extreme in their self-proclaimed wokeness; people who like grand-standing and virtue-signalling, and around whom the whiff of narcissism is strong'.

However slippery a term it may be, if it's taken to mean a desire to avoid giving offence to particular groups, it could certainly be argued that it's had an impact both on the briefs that cartoonists are given and on their approach to their work. Steve Bright, for one, has noticed how newspaper editors are now more wary than they once were of causing upset. 'Usually,' he says, 'we'll discuss any potential of that happening at the "ideas" stage, before a line is drawn, and ideas are either dumped or tweaked or I spend a bit of time reassuring the editor of the day that I had no intention of drawing the bit they feared I might be drawing. So, we head it off at the pass mostly. I think in recent years there have been only two cartoons I've drawn to completion that didn't make it into the following day's paper.' Christian Adams, while pointing out that there have been only one or two occasions on which he has been advised to change a cartoon, notes that, among other things, 'Jokes about mental health and disability have to be handled carefully. I once described Theresa May as "cuckoo" (the image was a clock),' he goes on, 'and was advised not to use that word by my editor.' Physical features and stereotypes traditionally associated with particular groups require careful thought. Nicola Jennings told me that at the *Guardian* they have occasionally asked her 'to reduce the size of a nose or darken/lighten someone's skin colour' in order not to offend Jewish or Black people. At *The Times*, Morten Morland has occasionally drawn criticism for the way he draws Diane Abbott or Priti Patel. 'It's usually because they disagree with the cartoon itself,' he says, 'and need something to hit back with. So, by hinting that the caricature is racist they aim to discredit the whole cartoon.'

This cartoon by Cecil Orr was published in the *Daily Record* on 24 February 1939. The caption reads 'The B.B.C. is taking further precautions to prevent offensive jokes getting on the air.'

Contemporary cartoonists are particularly nervous about getting involved in debates about transgender people and transgender rights, arguing that whatever a cartoonist comes up with is likely to invite fierce condemnation from one side or another. They are all too aware of the experience of Stella Perrett at the *Morning Star* when she ventured to draw a cartoon on the subject of transitioning that featured a crocodile telling several worried newts, 'Don't worry your pretty little heads! I'm transitioning as a newt!' To her mind it was 'a literal comment on the very real, physical, fear women and girls feel at the prospect of entire men being allowed into "Women-only" spaces', but, although it was published, such was the backlash on social media (columnist Owen Jones described the cartoon as 'vicious') that the newspaper published an apology (without informing Perrett first). The cartoonist was also contacted by the police after the cartoon was reported as a 'hate crime'.

Not surprisingly, then, when it comes to particularly contentious issues, many cartoonists tend to self-censor. 'I think cartoonists should be free to comment, but obviously you have to think about what you are saying,' says Steve Bell, whose own cartoons have landed him in hot water on several occasions. 'You don't just blow out the first thing that comes into your head, you consider what

Stella Perrett's cartoon was published in the *Morning Star* on 18 February 2020. The newspaper apologised 'unreservedly' for featuring the cartoon after much criticism.

you are saying. That can be difficult.' Andy Davey says that when it comes to debates about diversity, 'I have never experienced any censorship on the matter' but that's 'largely because I steer clear of the subject'. He is, in any case, sceptical about the so-called 'culture wars', which he regards as 'a deliberate distraction from the more important issues afflicting our society – poverty, inequality, government corruption, hypocrisy and lies, the influence of big money and more'. Dave Brown follows the same line: 'I prefer to concentrate my fire on recognisable individual politicians and try to avoid drawing figures representing groups of people, which might result in stereotyping.'

This is understandable, but it does lead to a certain paradox. Contemporary cartoonists want to avoid causing offence, but they are doing so in a profession whose roots lie in shock and outrage. David English, the editor of the *Daily Mail* between 1971 and 1992, stated in his newspaper that cartoonists in Britain had earned the freedom to ridicule and target whoever they felt deserved their vitriolic attention. 'No one in public life can expect to escape their remorseless eye,' he argued. 'Yes they are often cruel, yes, they are often unfair! Yes, they can turn a gentle caricature into a grotesque gargoyle. Yet without them, how impoverished would we be. For the cartoonist, given that very special licence which British society has granted him over the centuries, is able to say things through his drawings which the rest of us only dare whisper. Of course the cartoonist's work is invariably offensive to his victim.' English, it need hardly be pointed out, worked for a right-wing newspaper. But his views on this topic are ones shared by those whose political loyalties are very different. 'Of course as a cartoonist I work on that margin of what is acceptable,' says the *Independent*'s Dave Brown; 'the cartoon needs to unsettle and discomfort the reader a little if it is to penetrate the target and not simply bounce off.'

Dutch cartoonist Tjeerd Royaards expresses the internal conflict that many in his profession now feel:

Most cartoonists like to see themselves on the side of the oppressed. In short, most consider themselves to be woke. But cartoonists also like to see themselves as champions of freedom of expression. And this is where tension arises. Because being woke has at times evolved into cancel culture, with large groups of people protesting . . . or going after people with certain opinions on social media, with the purpose of censoring or publicly humiliating these individuals. And cartoonists have not been spared this fate; often using stereotypes as part of our visual language, the way we portray certain groups or ethnicities in our work has sparked numerous incidents in the past few years.

Peter Brookes expresses the uncertainty that many of his cartooning colleagues currently feel: 'On the diversity and woke thing, it is difficult to define a clear position because there are too many aspects to it. Some people are no longer talking about it while others get fired up on it. Also your own mind changes over time.' He personally feels that 'cartoons ought to reflect what is going on in society', adding 'all you have to do is look at television adverts and everyone is a mixed-race family, you don't see White or Black families'. But, in the current environment, trying to do the 'right' thing can sometimes be problematic. At *Private Eye*, there has been a move to ensure that the cartoonists who contribute include people from diverse backgrounds in their work. One cartoonist, who did not want to be named, told me that they were asked to change the race of one of the figures in a cartoon even though doing so undermined the gag, and that they felt uncomfortable doing so.

Of course, part of the issue here is that British cartoonists still tend to be white and male. This, the *Sunday Times*'s Nick Newman says, 'can make any joke about ethnicity feel awkward or patronising. Cartoonists may be cowards, but we are not afraid to admit to our cowardice in avoiding the issue.' He goes on:

Nowadays readers often write to publications complaining about the dearth of ethnic minorities in our drawings and demand for cartoons to be more inclusive. It's like being trapped in a bad political cartoon, walking a tightrope above a minefield. Cartoons involve laughing at someone. If that person is Black, you risk appearing racist; even including a BAME character in the background of a drawing can lead to accusations of tokenism ('background box-tickers'). Including any minority character in a cartoon can run the risk of implying that the cartoon is about race and so can inadvertently politicise the cartoon. At the end of the day, it's safer to make the pale, male and stale the butt of the joke.

Nick Newman created this pocket cartoon for the *Spectator*, 11 September 2021.

Patrick Blower agrees:

We're not that far off a point where cartoonists will only be able to lampoon white, public school-educated, biologically-born males. Even as Britain becomes more and more ethnically diverse, satirical drawings will increasingly resemble an all-white Giles crowd scene from the 1950s. I feel we're regressing as we all have to bow to the tyranny of identity politics and the pyramid of privilege where everyone apart from the designated groups at the top are accorded protected status.

There's inevitably a generational aspect to all this. As a rule, those under 60 tend to view concerns about wokeness as a fuss about nothing, while those over 60 view wokeness as an unreasonable constraint. After all, they have experienced a world that, for good or ill, was very different from today's. It all reminds me of what the distinctly non-establishment cartoonist David Low's widow, Madeline, wrote to the American cartoonist Draper Hill in 1969. 'If you come to England, you will see a great difference not only in the horrid tall buildings, but in the attitude of the people. I often wonder what David would think of the political situation and of the PERMISSIVE SOCIETY.' Such opinions would most likely have been common among her age group. One wonders what she would have thought of today's social mores.

My own view is that if newspapers want to see the best cartoons produced, they should employ the best cartoonists, whatever their background, and then allow them the freedom to follow the American humourist and writer Finley Peter Dunne's 1902 injunction to 'comfort the afflicted and afflict the comfortable' without too many constraints. As an unrepentant Patrick Blower comments, 'Bring back the rude times!'

THE CARTOONS

The adaptable Grant Shapps achieved his fifth cabinet post in less than 12 months, when Prime Minister Rishi Sunak transferred him from the energy security portfolio to defence, after Ben Wallace stood down. But Lord Dannatt, a former British Army chief of the general staff, worried that Shapps 'knew very little' about military matters. The cartoonist evokes the satirical-apocalyptic magazine *MAD* and its boyish cover character Alfred E. Neuman, whose catchphrase is 'What, me worry?' He also invokes 'Michael Green', the controversial persona used by Shapps in his former web-based commercial enterprises, and 'Sebastian Fox', an unidentified provider of testimonials for Shapps's business.

1 September 2023
Dave Brown
Independent

On the eve of the new school year, a government directive suddenly ordered the closure of English school buildings thought to be at structural risk on account of the 'reinforced auto-clave aerated concrete' (RAAC) – nicknamed 'Aero Bar' – used in their construction. The number of schools affected by what the BBC called 'bubbly concrete' was unclear, with the broadcaster estimating at least 156. Within days, Sunak would be denying that when he was chancellor, his inadequate funding had worsened the problem. RAAC has an estimated lifespan of 30 years. Polls suggested that the lifespan of the Conservative government was reaching its final year.

2 September 2023
Rob Murray
Daily Telegraph

7 September 2023
Steve Bell
Guardian

Prince Andrew gave up royal duties in 2019, following the fallout of his friendship with disgraced US financier Jeffrey Epstein. However, in late August 2023 Andrew was invited to join King Charles and Queen Camilla at the Balmoral Estate, suggesting, to royal watchers, a thaw in the royal siblings' relations. A few days later it emerged that documents relating to Andrew's trips during his 10-year stint as UK 'special representative' for trade would be kept secret for another 42 years, until 2065. The revelation followed the biographer Andrew Lownie's attempt to access the documents via a Freedom of Information request.

On 4 September, Education Secretary Gillian Keegan visited an Essex school affected by RAAC construction deficiencies. She became a focal point of the controversy, not only because of her job but because of recent remarks made when she thought she was off air. Concluding a televised interview with ITV News's Daniel Hewitt, she exclaimed: 'Does anyone ever say, "You know what, you've done a fucking good job because everyone else has sat on their arse and done nothing"?' A spokesman for Rishi Sunak called the remarks 'unacceptable'. It was not clear whether they were aimed at fellow politicians, the media, or both.

8 September 2023
Graeme Bandeira
Northern Agenda

Following the wide circulation of a TikTok video showing an American XL bully dog attacking a child and an adult in Birmingham, Home Secretary Suella Braverman made her feelings known. She took to the social media platform X (formerly Twitter), called the incident 'appalling', and described XL bullies, which are related to pit-bull terriers, as 'a clear and lethal danger to our communities, particularly children'. 'I have', she stated, 'commissioned urgent advice on banning them' – and so adding them to the existing four breeds of dog banned in the UK.

12 September 2023
Morten Morland
The Times

Differences in personalities and politics at the top of the Labour Party continued to suggest some divergences in mapping the way ahead. While Sir Keir Starmer reshuffled his front-bench team and looked to winning over the middle ground, his deputy, Angela Rayner, honed her more left-leaning reputation. She told the Trades Union Congress (TUC) that she would 'not let down' the unions, contrasting Labour's plans for improving employment rights and banning zero-hours contracts with 'this government's version of levelling up', which she called 'a sham – and a scam'.

13 September 2023
Patrick Blower
Daily Telegraph

LITTLE ROCKET MEN

Blower 14.9.23

AFTER DR. STRANGELOVE

14 September 2023
Patrick Blower
Daily Telegraph

On 13 September, North Korean leader Kim Jong-un was at Russia's Vostochny Cosmodrome, in eastern Siberia, for a summit with Vladimir Putin. While Kim promised unconditional support for Russia's 'sacred fight' in Ukraine, Putin told reporters that Kim shows 'great interest' in rocket technology. Western analysts concluded that Kim was seeking Russian space and submarine technology while Putin was interested in possible arms supplies across the North Korean border. Donald Trump had belittled Kim as 'little rocket man' in 2017, while in the blackly comic Cold War film *Dr. Strangelove* (1964), the gung-ho Major Kong joyously straddles a nuclear bomb as it falls.

In a tweet featuring the *Daily Telegraph* headline 'Starmer plots deal to take EU migrants', Suella Braverman claimed that Sir Keir Starmer would 'agree to make Britain the dumping ground for many of the millions of illegal migrants that Europe doesn't want'. As the cartoonist saw it, 'The pot's calling the kettle black, because [this] is really what she's done. Although I'm not against that, because I don't see migrants in the same way that she does – we can take more than she'd ever admit were possible.' He added: 'I rather feel I shall be drawing Starmer a lot during the next year.'

15 September 2023
Peter Brookes
The Times

In his newspaper, the *Sun*'s Trevor Kavanagh wrote that Sir Keir Starmer 'will end illegal migration by essentially making it legal. He will stitch up a "repatriation" deal with Emmanuel Macron, who is waiting like a Bully XL dog to rip off the hand that already feeds him. And he will magically smash the "evil people smugglers"'. Starmer was, in Kavanagh's view, 'either "delusional", as an EU official described him last week, or thinks we are all stupid'. Starmer had written in the *Sun* that Labour, in government, would abandon Conservative 'gimmicks' and create a new security force for 'breaking up the smugglers' business model'.

18 September 2023
Steve Bright
Sun

Following investigations by *The Times*, *Sunday Times* and Channel 4, on 16 September the media published allegations of rape and sexual assault made by four women against the comedian Russell Brand. That evening, Brand went on stage for his scheduled performance at Wembley Park's Troubadour venue, London, in front of welcoming fans. While alluding to 'things that I absolutely cannot talk about', he told the crowd: 'I really appreciate your support.'

The alleged offences took place in 2006–13, during Brand's peak period of fame. He insisted that all his sexual encounters were consensual.

18 September 2023
Ella Baron
The Times

22 September 2023
Dave Brown
Independent

Rishi Sunak relaxed the UK's carbon-emission timetable for reaching Net Zero, pleading 'the impact on families' in terms of costs as his motive. A ban on new petrol and diesel cars was delayed five years, to 2035, and there were new exemptions to forthcoming bans on installing gas and oil boilers. Some critics accused Sunak of abandoning measures to combat climate change in favour of a short-term electoral boost. In the comedy film *Blazing Saddles* (1974), the African-American sheriff of a racist town gets out of a scrape by holding a gun to his head and retreating, as the gullible crowd believes he is being taken hostage.

Between the Brexit Referendum (2016) and the UK's exit from the European Union in 2020, the Liberal Democrats remained opposed to Brexit. But now, party leader Sir Ed Davey asserted that rejoining the EU was 'off the table'. In what was interpreted as an effort not to alienate former Leave voters, he preferred to emphasise issues such as GP waiting times and water companies' discharging of sewage into UK waterways and seas. But some Liberal Democrats like Caroline Voaden, the parliamentary candidate for Totnes, wanted 'to see the party being more honest and braver about addressing the elephant in the room'.

22 September 2023
Andy Davey
Evening Standard

23 September 2023
Ben Jennings
Guardian

It seemed the end of an era when the 92-year-old media tycoon Rupert Murdoch announced his retirement as chairman of Fox and News Corp, with the roles passing to his son, Lachlan. Nevertheless, Murdoch planned to continue as 'chairman emeritus' and promised to 'be here to participate' in the challenges of the future. Despite the optimism, Fox News was burdened with expensive lawsuits, because of suggestions in its coverage of the 2020 US presidential elections that voting machines had been inaccurate: one manufacturer, Dominion, had won a settlement of $787.5 million; another, Smartmatic, was seeking more than three times that much.

NEW LINE OF DUTY

Suella Braverman ordered a review of armed policing, after a number of Metropolitan Police handed in their firearms permits, fearful of ending up on the wrong side of the law. A catalyst was the charge of 'murder' brought against an armed officer after the fatal shooting of the unarmed Chris Kaba in September 2022. The Home Office now responded with a request to the Ministry of Defence for armed support – should it be needed – in the Met's counter-terrorism operations. Meanwhile, Braverman, tweeting in officers' defence, insisted that 'they have to make split-second decisions under extraordinary pressures'.

25 September 2023
David Simonds
Evening Standard

25 September 2023
Patrick Blower
Daily Telegraph

Just before the 2023 Conservative Party conference opened, rumours swirled that Rishi Sunak, under Treasury pressure, would abandon the northern leg of the HS2 high-speed rail line between Birmingham and Manchester. Business leaders, regional politicians and ex-prime ministers, including Boris Johnson and David Cameron, weighed in to oppose the move. Since March 2023, Sunak had often spoken to the press from behind a lectern emblazoned with the slogan 'Stop the Boats', referring to illegal migrants.

THE STUFF YOU WON'T HEAR ANYWHERE ELSE

Because it's such utter rubbish

GB News fell foul of media regulator Ofcom following an edition of the *Dan Wootton Tonight* show featuring fellow presenter (and 'actor-turned-activist') Laurence Fox. Responding to comments about male suicide made elsewhere by journalist Ava Evans (also known as Ava Santini), Fox launched a tirade of disparaging remarks, including: 'Show me a single self-respecting man that would like to climb into bed with that woman.' Ofcom found the comments 'misogynistic', 'potentially highly offensive' and 'not sufficiently challenged', concluding that there were 'significant concerns' about GB News. The broadcaster, which also employed Nigel Farage and Conservative MP Lee Anderson as presenters, suspended Wootton and Fox.

29 September 2023
Ben Jennings
Guardian

30 September 2023
Peter Brookes
The Times

On the night of 27/28 September, Northumberland lost a landmark when a famous sycamore tree was illegally felled. The cartoonist felt that 'It was so outrageous when the Sycamore Gap tree at Hadrian's Wall was cut down – an absolute scandal. The tree was a wonderful symbol, and unmissable, really, to use as a metaphor. So, I had the Tory tree again, and Labour chopping it down. Not many mourners for that, but there were for the actual tree.'

Rishi Sunak was a self-avowed 'huge' fan of the *Star Wars* film franchise. While speaking to BBC Three Counties Radio – whose area of coverage includes Pinewood Studios – he joked that 'if they could get me a cameo . . . and I would get to say "Red Seven standing by" before we take down the Death Star, that would make me a very happy man'. As the cartoonist explained, it was Sunak's ' "childhood dream" to pilot an X-wing aircraft. He was said to be planning to announce measures to drive a wedge between his party and Labour, but the polls were still bad. Can he destroy the evil Death Starmer?'

1 October 2023
Andy Davey
Sunday Telegraph

On 2 October, the second day of the Conservative Party conference in Manchester, it was Rishi Sunak's short-lived predecessor at Number 10 who basked in the spotlight. 'Let's stop taxing and banning things, and start producing and buildings things,' Liz Truss urged a packed gathering at the 'Great British Growth Rally'. Truss had ignored calls to stay away and not embarrass the prime minister. Instead, this oversubscribed fringe event had queues trying to get in. By contrast, party managers were reportedly trying to pack the sparsely attended main auditorium with aides, to improve the television footage.

3 October 2023
Patrick Blower
Daily Telegraph

When Rishi Sunak gave his closing speech at the Conservative Party conference, he confirmed speculation that the government was binning the Birmingham–Manchester leg of HS2. Its £36 billion of funding would instead be earmarked for a wide array of smaller transport projects across the English North and Midlands. Audaciously, despite 13 years of Conservative government, Sunak billed himself as the man who represented change from a tired consensus. He announced plans to overhaul the National Health Service (NHS) and A levels, and, most eye-catchingly, to ban anyone currently aged 14 from ever being able, legally, to buy tobacco.

5 October 2023
Steve Bell
Guardian

When it came to Sir Keir Starmer's closing speech at the Labour Party conference, in Liverpool, he first had to contend with an unexpected intervention. A protestor from a grassroots group called 'People Want Democracy' infiltrated the proceedings, clambered onto the stage and showered the leader of the opposition with glitter. On removing his glittery jacket and regaining his composure, Starmer told his audience: 'If he thinks that bothers me, he doesn't know me.' The media consensus was that, despite the potential life-threatening security breach, Starmer had managed to turn matters to his advantage.

11 October 2023
Christian Adams
Evening Standard

STATE OF INSECURITY...

On 7 October, fighters for the Palestinian Hamas movement (and allied militant groups) infiltrated Israel, from Gaza, and launched a shocking spree of killing and hostage-taking. As the cartoonist explained, the attack happened 'on a Saturday morning, but I wasn't down to do a cartoon until Thursday's paper. So everything had already been seen and commented on, and I had to find some other way of looking at it. When something major and horrendous like this happens, such as 9/11, you have to do something quite graphic and quite simple. So I decided to use the Israeli flag to illustrate the insecurity of what happened and show Hamas breaking through.'

12 October 2023
Peter Brookes
The Times

13 October 2023
Steven Camley
Scottish Herald

Dr Lisa Cameron – the Scottish Nationalist MP for East Kilbride, Strathaven and Lesmahagow – defected to the Scottish Conservatives just days before the results of a constituency selection contest revealed whether she could stand for the SNP at the next general election. Describing the Scottish Nationalist Party (SNP) as 'bad for my health', the socially conservative Cameron blamed a 'toxic culture' and controversies surrounding the SNP's chief whip for her departure. Given that both the SNP and Conservatives had suffered heavy defeats in recent by-elections, it appeared to some that Dr Cameron was swapping one sinking ship for another.

The sheer scale of the Hamas-led attacks of 7 October, which resulted in about 1,200 civilian dead and more than 250 hostages taken, unleashed immediate Israeli air strikes on Gaza. On 8 October, Israel declared war on Hamas; by 9 October, 300,000 Israeli reservists were mobilised and by 13 October, Israel was warning civilians to evacuate Gaza City. Relatively quickly, Gaza's urban landscape was turning to ashen rubble. Israel's stated goals were to destroy Hamas and bring the hostages home – some of whom had been paraded in Gaza after their capture – but war also brought fears that hostages might become collateral damage.

14 October 2023
Nicola Jennings
Guardian

16 October 2023
Patrick Blower
Daily Telegraph

War in the Middle East had the effect of diverting Western media and political attention – and potentially economic and military aid – away from Ukraine's ongoing conflict with Russia. Initially silent after the 7 October Hamas attack, by 16 October Vladimir Putin was engaged in heavy phone diplomacy with Israeli Prime Minister Benjamin Netanyahu and the leaders of neighbouring countries, as he sought what the Kremlin described as 'an early ceasefire and the establishment of a humanitarian truce'. In the wake of the Ukraine War, the image of Putin as peacemaker carried considerable irony.

ALL BEHIND YOU, BIBI

On 9 October, the leaders of the UK, United States, Germany, France and Italy declared 'steadfast and united support of Israel' and backed Israel's 'efforts to defend itself'. But the mounting Palestinian death toll and physical destruction of Gaza was putting pressure on such unqualified support. As President Biden arrived in Israel, he reminded his hosts: 'After 9/11, we were enraged in the United States. While we sought justice and got justice, we also made mistakes.' The cartoonist reimagines David Low's 1940 wartime cartoon of patriotic unity, 'All behind you, Winston' – except that here, the backers of Netanyahu ('Bibi') are looking more fretful.

18 October 2023
Morten Morland
The Times

The United States was by far the most significant ally – in political, military and economic terms – of both Ukraine and Israel, two nations involved in full-blown war. Would its resources and political capital stretch sufficiently to both geopolitical crises? To add to US burdens, there was the ever-present challenge of Xi Jinping's rising China, with its expanded military capabilities and its increasingly bellicose attitude towards Taiwan, whose security was also underwritten by the United States. That burden seemed to be getting heavier as Vladimir Putin attended an international summit in Beijing, welcomed by Xi as his 'dear friend'.

18 October 2023
Patrick Blower
Daily Telegraph

Sir Keir Starmer proclaimed that his party was 'redrawing the political map' when, on 19 October, very large swings to Labour in by-elections gifted them two 'safe' Conservative seats. According to the polling guru Professor Sir John Curtice, the 23.9 per cent swing in Tamworth was the 'second highest in post-war by-election history', while in Mid-Bedfordshire the Conservative vote-share fell even more steeply. Yet Andrew Bowie, the secretary for energy security, insisted to Sky News that the government was 'on the right course', while Rishi Sunak, admitting the by-elections were 'disappointing', indicated no change of direction.

22 October 2023
Chris Riddell
Observer

Tensions between the Home Office and Metropolitan Police Commissioner Sir Mark Rowley emerged following an anti-Israel, pro-Gaza demonstration in London (21 October). Some protestors chanted 'jihad', and a 'source close to' Suella Braverman indicated that she wanted to know why no police action was taken, since 'there can be no room for incitement to hatred'. Sir Mark responded that the law gave the police no powers to arrest in such a case, where interpreting 'jihad' involved questions of 'taste and decency'. He insisted: 'The conversation finished around the line of the law. It's our job to enforce that line. It's Parliament's job to draw that line.'

24 October 2023
Christian Adams
Evening Standard

Despite the worsening humanitarian situation in Gaza, the Labour Party's official line supported the government in resisting calls for an Israeli ceasefire, on the basis that Israel was exercising its right of self-defence. But there were consequences for party unity, as Starmer faced anger particularly from his Muslim MPs and MPs representing communities sympathetic to Gaza's civilians. According to the cartoonist, 'There's something about this cartoon which had *me* sitting on the fence too. Is he *sitting* on the fence, or is he painfully pierced by it? I remember feeling ambivalent about it while drawing it. Maybe that's just as well.'

26 October 2023
Peter Schrank
The Times

On 27 October, controversial gatherings took place in Moscow. Iran's deputy foreign minister, Ali Bagheri Kani, met with his Russian opposite number, Mikhail Bogdanov, to discuss the war in Gaza. They also met with Abu Marzouk, described by Russia's Tass News Agency as 'a senior political leader' of Hamas. Abu Marzouk complimented Russia on inviting his movement's leadership, declaring that it demonstrated that Hamas was a 'national liberation movement' rather than a terrorist group. By contrast, the Israeli foreign ministry called Russia's invitation to Hamas representatives 'obscene'. According to the cartoonist, 'Putin's circle of influence shrank but became progressively more provocative and threatening to the West.'

28 October 2023
Andy Davey
Daily Telegraph

Having already submitted a 114-page 'statement of evidence' to the UK Covid-19 Inquiry, Dominic Cummings, who had been Boris Johnson's 'Adviser to the Prime Minister', now appeared in person. In his characteristically blunt style, he painted a picture of chaos and confusion in government during spring 2020, as Johnson struggled to face the realities of the emerging pandemic. It was, Cummings felt, the 'wrong crisis' for the 'skill set' of a prime minister who (according to Cummings) was called 'the trolley' behind his back, because he veered from opinion to opinion. On 13 November 2021, Johnson fired Cummings. They had, Cummings attested, not spoken since.

31 October 2023
Christian Adams
Evening Standard

On 1–2 November, the UK hosted an international Artificial Intelligence (AI) Safety Summit at Bletchley Park, Buckinghamshire. It drew together political and business leaders with academics to consider threats to 'global safety' and risks such as those from 'unpredictable advances' in technology (including 'loss of control'). Rishi Sunak warned that while AI could bring transformational benefits, its dangers were comparable to 'pandemics and nuclear war'. The 28 nations represented (including the United States and China) agreed a 'Bletchley Declaration', whereby they would cooperate on safety research. But sceptics feared that national self-interest would still rear its head.

3 November 2023
Kevin Kallaugher
Economist

Following another 'day of action' against the war in Gaza, some press reports alleged that volunteers selling poppies, as part of the annual Royal British Legion fundraising appeal, had been intimidated. At London's Charing Cross station, a poppy-seller was, according to the *Daily Express*, 'surrounded'; at Edinburgh's Waverley station, a veteran was assaulted, according to the *Daily Mail*. The minister for veterans' affairs, Johnny Mercer, tweeted that he would be happy to 'rattle a tin' with beleaguered poppy-sellers. But the British Transport Police, finding no evidence for the incidents, criticised 'misleading information' in the 'mainstream media' for making poppy-sellers fearful.

6 November 2023
Patrick Blower
Daily Telegraph

The journalist Michael Crick issued a tweet claiming that a GB News producer had thrown him off a live discussion (4 November) of media censorship, after he had lambasted the channel for right-wing bias. Crick, who thought that Ofcom should simply 'shut down' GB News, thought it 'absurd' that the broadcaster fielded 'Tory MP, after Tory MP, after Tory MP', continuing his criticism as presenter Neil Oliver tried to cut to a break. According to the cartoonist, the idea for his image came after 'a bit of back and forth' with his editor, Jack Peat, 'before we landed on Crick being gagged by a GB News mic'.

6 November 2023
Fergus Boylan
London Economic

On 7 November, at the annual State Opening of Parliament, King Charles presented the government's legislative agenda in his first King's Speech. The 21 bills, some in progress, covered topics such as increased prison sentences for sadistic murders, ending leasehold status for new houses, and awarding new licences for oil and gas operations in the North Sea. Commentators scrutinised the king's tone of voice – more expressive than his mother's – for any clues as to his feelings over the words he had to speak. The *Daily Mirror*'s Kevin Maguire wrote: 'No wonder Charlie curled his lip . . . you wait decades to inherit Mummy's job then they hand you drivel.'

7 November 2023
Dave Brown
Independent

8 November 2023
Christian Adams
Evening Standard

On 8 November, as arguments about pro-Palestinian protests and their policing rumbled on, Labour MP Imran Hussain resigned from Sir Keir Starmer's front bench over the party's refusal to call for a ceasefire in Gaza. More worrying was the speculation that up to a dozen other members of Labour's shadow cabinet were on the verge of stepping down too. Starmer stuck to his line that a ceasefire now would only 'embolden' Hamas, though he backed a 'humanitarian pause'. On 16 November, 10 Labour front benchers resigned their roles to vote for an (unsuccessful) SNP amendment on the King's Speech backing a ceasefire.

As Rishi Sunak condemned a 'disrespectful' anti-war march planned for Armistice Day (11 November), his home secretary took to *The Times* to accuse the Metropolitan Police of bias. She had already characterised anti-war protestors as 'hate marchers'. Now she claimed that the police gave a 'stern response' to right-wing protests but 'largely ignored' protests by 'pro-Palestinian mobs . . . even when clearly breaking the law'. Calls for Suella Braverman's resignation intensified. The cartoonist noted, 'it was widely thought that she'd be gone by the end of the day, so I had to do something that would work if she was out, but also if she was still there'.

10 November 2023
Peter Brookes
The Times

As pressure mounted for Suella Braverman's dismissal, Rishi Sunak declared there would be an internal investigation into why her *Times* article – which accused the police of 'playing favourites' – did not include the changes stipulated by his office. This controversy came hot on the heels of Braverman's recent proposals, amid a crisis in services for the homeless, to crack down on rough-sleeping. She had tweeted, 'we cannot allow our streets to be taken over by rows of tents occupied by people, many of them from abroad, living on the streets as a lifestyle choice'. On 13 November, Sunak fired Braverman.

12 November 2023
Chris Riddell
Observer

The most surprising appointment in the cabinet reshuffle following Braverman's dismissal was making ex-prime minister (Lord) David Cameron the new foreign secretary. Soon, he was in Kiev, meeting President Zelensky. According to the cartoonist, 'The point I was making here was that, because of Israel and Gaza, the focus has moved from Ukraine. So Zelensky is comparing his lot with Cameron's before he came back – feeling lost or forgotten. I've enjoyed being able to focus on Cameron again. He's still got his hair, which is important because I always drew him with a little plume of hair at the top.'

17 November 2023
Peter Brookes
The Times

On 15 November, the UK Supreme Court declared the plan to send asylum-seekers to Rwanda, for processing, 'unlawful'. Out of office, Suella Braverman relayed her views in the *Daily Telegraph*, calling for a beefing-up of the Illegal Migration Act, an end to 'self-deception and spin' and 'no more magical thinking'. Meanwhile, Sunak announced money for local roads. As the cartoonist explained, 'Sunak has set out how £8.3 billion of promised funding – over the next eleven years! – will be used to tackle what he called the "scourge of potholes". Councils say it's not enough. Meanwhile, Braverman said that Sunak's "tinkering" is not enough to sort out the Rwanda plan.'

18 November 2023
Andy Davey
Daily Telegraph

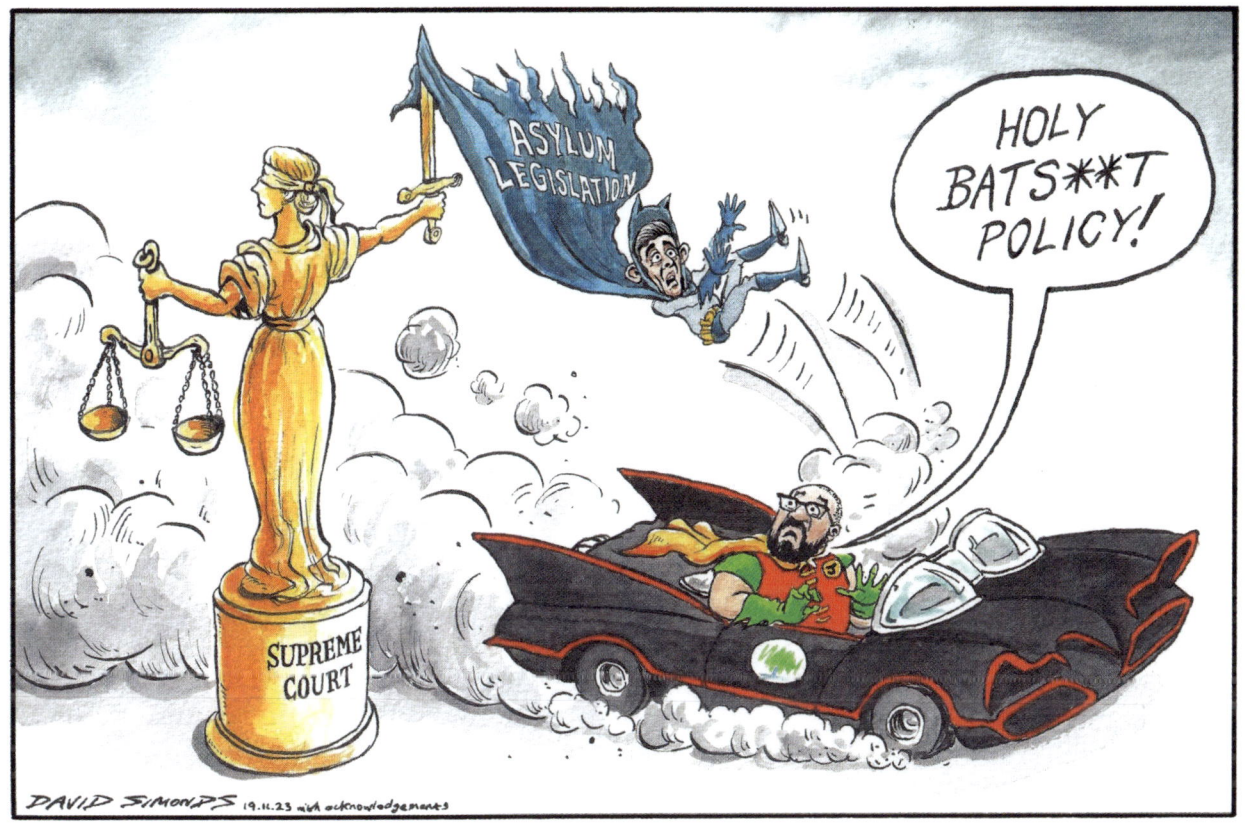

In declaring the Rwanda policy 'unlawful', the UK Supreme Court upheld an Appeal Court ruling: that the government could not guarantee that asylum-seekers' human rights would be respected in Rwanda. Rishi Sunak insisted that the government would now seek a new treaty with Rwanda and bring in emergency legislation to declare Rwanda 'safe'. It fell to the new home secretary, James Cleverly, to defend the stance. He told interviewers he could not 'recall' privately describing the Rwanda policy as 'batshit'. In the 1960s' US TV show *Batman*, based on the DC Comics hero, sidekick Robin frequently invoked 'holy' to register alarm.

19 November 2023
David Simonds
Evening Standard

23 November 2023
Ben Jennings
Guardian

Critics of Chancellor Jeremy Hunt's Autumn Statement (22 November) felt that his self-proclaimed 'biggest package of tax cuts since the 1980s' lulled the public into a false sense of security. The headline measures promised reductions in National Insurance, rises in benefits and pensions, tax breaks on company expenses, and extensions to Covid-19-era rate rebates for shops and hospitality businesses. But the measures were announced against the background of the highest tax burden in 70 years. Significantly, there was no rise in the £12,570 earnings threshold at which income tax began. In some analyses, the give-aways were wiped out by 'stealth' taxation.

OCTOBER 2021

JUNE 2023

NOVEMBER 2023

In 2021, Shadow Chancellor Rachel Reeves had announced a 'Green Prosperity Plan', whereby Labour, in power, would borrow to invest £28 billion annually in transforming the UK's energy for a green future. By June 2023, amid rising borrowing costs, she pleaded that 'financial stability has to come first' and, as the cartoonist commented, she 'watered down Labour's "green pledge", saying the figure would not be reached until 2027'. By late November, amid rumours of intense discussion within Labour, there was much speculation that, as the cartoonist said, 'it would probably not be reached at all'.

26 November 2023
Andy Davey
Daily Telegraph

27 November 2023
Christian Adams
Evening Standard

According to details emerging from a controversial new book about the Royal Family – *Endgame* by Omid Scobie – King Charles was visibly angered by comments and accusations made by Prince Harry in the previous year's documentary series *Harry and Meghan*. Scobie claimed that a palace aide had confided that the King 'went from not wanting to talk about his son to openly criticizing "that fool"'. Scobie had already published *Finding Freedom: Harry and Meghan and the Making of a Modern Royal Family* in 2020, the year the couple settled in California.

On 19 November, TV viewers saw Reform UK's 'honorary president', Nigel Farage, join other celebrities for the annual series of stomach-churning challenges comprising *I'm a Celebrity . . . Get Me Out of Here!* He had entered, hoping to show he was not 'mean-spirited, small-minded, nasty' and, despite past injuries, he insisted 'I can still do most things'. 'It's in for a penny, in for a pound,' he said. In fact, it was in for a reported fee of £1.5 million. In early November, a poll by Conservative Home suggested that 70 per cent of Conservative Party members would be happy with Farage as their leader.

27 November 2023
Steve Bright
Sun

LOSING HIS MARBLES..?

29 November 2023
Dave Brown
Independent

During an interview with the BBC's Laura Kuenssberg, the Greek prime minister, Kyriakos Mitsotakis, spoke about wanting the British Museum's Parthenon sculptures (the Elgin Marbles) returned to Athens. Two days later, his scheduled meeting with Rishi Sunak was abruptly cancelled. Sunak claimed that Mitsotakis was in breach of a promise not to lobby publicly on the issue. In Parliament, Sir Keir Starmer quipped, 'Never mind the museum, it's the prime minister who has obviously lost his marbles.' Meanwhile, Business Secretary Kemi Badenoch put pressure on Sunak for 'much, much tougher measures' to control immigration.

On 30 November, the former health secretary, Matt Hancock, appeared at the UK Covid-19 Inquiry. He argued that had his advice for an earlier initial lockdown been heeded, Covid-related deaths in that phase might have been reduced by 90 per cent. Yet, other witnesses criticised Hancock as overconfident and underperforming. He resigned in June 2021, after video footage showed the married minister kissing his aide and girlfriend Gina Coladangelo, thus breaching social distancing rules. In 2021, the political activist group Led By Donkeys collaborated with the Covid-19 Bereaved Families for Justice on a Thames-side memorial wall, opposite Parliament, adorned with more than 220,000 painted hearts.

1 December 2023
Ben Jennings
Guardian

The latest UN 'Conference of the Parties' addressing climate change, COP28, was hosted in Dubai. As the cartoonist explained, 'David Cameron and Rishi Sunak were there . . . I'm pointing out Cameron's less than squeaky-clean past. He may well do good things as foreign secretary, but his comeback has reignited interest in the Greensill scandal.' In 2020, Cameron had lobbied ministers (principally Sunak as chancellor) and civil servants to deploy the firm Greensill Capital, in which he held shares, for 'supply side finance'. The offer was not taken up. Greensill collapsed, insolvent, in 2021, after which a Treasury select committee found Cameron guilty of 'a significant lack of judgement'.

2 December 2023
Peter Brookes
The Times

HANDBAGGED

The Daily Telegraph

Starmer appeals to the Right

Blowe 4·12·23

Writing in the *Sunday Telegraph* (3 December), Sir Keir Starmer complimented the achievements of his Labour predecessors Clement Attlee and Tony Blair; but it was his praise for Margaret Thatcher that attracted headlines. She had, he wrote, 'sought to drag Britain out of its stupor by setting loose our natural entrepreneurialism'. It was an explicit attempt to woo disappointed Conservative voters, to whom, as Starmer wrote, 'my party extends the hand of friendship'. Starmer's invocation of the handbag-wielding Thatcher – notwithstanding his caveats that he did not agree with all her policies – produced some grumbles within Labour ranks.

4 December 2023
Patrick Blower
Daily Telegraph

In the aftermath of the UK Supreme Court's Rwanda decision, James Cleverly flew to Kigali to sign a revised treaty and, in theory, 'stop the boats'. It was, he maintained, 'the strongest possible agreement', going 'far beyond' agreements reached by the United Nations High Commissioner for Refugees (UNHCR). Cleverly also insisted that Rwanda cared 'deeply about the rights of refugees'. *Wonka*, a prequel to the film *Willy Wonka & the Chocolate Factory* (1971; based on Roald Dahl's children's novels), had just opened. It revived Gene Wilder's song from the earlier film, with the lyrics 'Come with me and you'll be / in a world of pure imagination'.

5 December 2023
Christian Adams
Evening Standard

It was now Boris Johnson's turn to give evidence at the UK Covid-19 Inquiry. He began with words of regret about 'the loss and suffering' endured by the British public, amid protests from some bereaved relatives shouting 'the dead can't hear your apologies'. Johnson defended the timing of the first lockdown on the basis of what was known about the disease by March 2020, even if, in hindsight, 'we should perhaps' have locked down earlier. In his view, 'the entire Whitehall establishment, scientific community included' badly underestimated the speed and scale of the pandemic. The BBC put the UK's Covid-related death toll (to mid-2023) at around 270,000.

7 December 2023
Ella Baron
Guardian

14 December 2023
Patrick Blower
Daily Telegraph

Just under 84,000 delegates attended COP28 in the United Arab Emirates (UAE) – double the size of the UK-hosted COP26. Some criticised the event as becoming more and more like a trade fair. King Charles, Rishi Sunak and David Cameron were just three of those who travelled there by private jet. The United Nations stressed that the event would need to achieve 'carbon neutrality', and the UAE promised to offset attendees' greenhouse gas emissions. The academics who wrote the article 'Navigating the Climate Conferences' (16 October 2023) put a private jet's carbon footprint at nine times that of a commercial plane.

In Brussels, Hungary's hard-line prime minister, Viktor Orbán, exercised his veto, scuppering his fellow EU leaders' desire to give Ukraine aid worth 50 billion euros. Earlier in December, in a diplomatic sleight of hand, he had temporarily left the discussions that then enabled the other 26 EU members to agree to talks with Ukraine about EU membership. But Hungary still maintained a close working relationship with Russia and, for now, was dependent on Russia for gas supplies. (Orbán eventually agreed to the aid package in March 2024, under some revised terms.)

17 December 2023
Morten Morland
The Times

In September 2023, Kiev's mayor, Vitali Klitschko, had reportedly asked London Mayor Sadiq Khan for any 4x4 vehicles and pickup trucks identified for 'scrappage' as part of a subsidised replacement scheme introduced for London's expanded Ultra Low Emissions Zone (ULEZ). As the cartoonist explained, in mid-December Khan 'rejected' the request as not legally possible under the scrappage subsidy terms – but attracted criticism that he was failing to support Ukraine. A week later, Khan joined the former Conservative defence secretary, Ben Wallace, in asking the transport secretary for a rule change to meet the Ukrainian request.

17 December 2023
Andy Davey
Daily Telegraph

In Israel, regular protests demanded 'Bring them home!' – referring to the hostages taken by Hamas and other militants during their incursion from Gaza on 7 October. However, the Israel Defense Forces admitted on 15 December that when fighting in the Shejaiya area of Gaza City, 'the IDF mistakenly identified three Israeli hostages as a threat' before killing them. The three men – Yotam Haim, Alon Shamriz and Samer El-Talalqa – had all been living on kibbutzes near the Gaza border when they were captured by Hamas. The IDF spoke of its 'deep remorse', while Benjamin Netanyahu called the incident an 'unbearable tragedy'.

18 December 2023
Nicola Jennings
Guardian

Rishi Sunak travelled to Rome to attend an annual summit of right-wing politicians and thinkers organised by the Italian prime minister, Giorgia Meloni, and her Brothers of Italy party. The two leaders had been building a friendly relationship, with shared views on migration. Sunak warned the summit that global rule changes were needed because 'if we do not tackle this problem . . . it will overwhelm our countries'. He also agreed funding with Meloni to tackle African migrants crossing from Tunisia. In the classic romantic comedy *Roman Holiday* (1953), the film's stars, Audrey Hepburn and Gregory Peck, zip around the city on a Vespa 125 scooter.

18 December 2023
Patrick Blower
Daily Telegraph

The ex-Conservative baroness Michelle Mone admitted to the BBC's Laura Kuenssberg that she had lied about a £200-million deal in which her husband's company, PPE Medpro, supplied personal protective equipment to the NHS during the Covid-19 pandemic. Lady Mone had helped get the company preferred status for contracts but had denied any financial benefit; she now admitted that she and her family were beneficiaries of trusts holding an estimated £60 million in profits. She denied that lying to the press was a crime. A widely circulated photograph had depicted Lady Mone on the couple's yacht, *Lady Michelle*.

19 December 2023
Ben Jennings
Guardian

In 2017, the Conservative government had set a target to build 300,000 new homes annually to tackle the housing crisis, and reiterated it in the party's 2019 general election manifesto. But, as Covid-19 struck, housebuilding declined and the target was never reached. Now, Michael Gove – as secretary for levelling up, housing and communities – announced house-building league tables for councils along with the threat of removing individual councils' planning powers if they opposed developments for no good reason. However, some exemptions remained, to retain the character of local environments and to exclude building on cities' green belts.

19 December 2023
Christian Adams
Evening Standard

Colorado's supreme court deployed a never-before-used section of the US Constitution's 14th amendment to ban Donald Trump from standing in that state's Republican Party primary election, ahead of the 2024 presidential race. In a 4–3 decision, the justices cited the Civil War-era clause – aimed at former Confederate secessionists – on account of Trump's 'call to his supporters to fight' on the day of the rioting and insurrection at the US Capitol (6 January 2021). Attacking the 'flawed' judgement, Trump's campaign team looked forward to the more conservative-leaning US Supreme Court reversing the ban.

21 December 2023
Dave Brown
Independent

On 19 December, the United States declared that it would gather an international naval force to protect commercial shipping on the vital sea lanes around the Horn of Africa and accessing the Suez Canal. The news came as an estimated 100 container ships had switched to sailing around southern Africa instead, adding 6,000 miles, more costs and several extra weeks to their journeys, all because of fear of Yemeni rebels' vessels, missiles and drones. The Iranian-backed Houthi rebels justified their attacks as a response to the war in Gaza, claiming that the ships targeted were somehow supplying Israel.

21 December 2023
Patrick Blower
Daily Telegraph

On 27 December, as winter storm Gerritt swept into the UK, the *Daily Telegraph* suggested that Jeremy Hunt was considering a dramatic reduction in inheritance tax at the next Budget. Although relatively few people paid inheritance tax because it only applied to estates worth at least £325,000 (and in many cases £500,000, or more), there was traditionally much support in Conservative circles for its reduction or even abolition. For its part, the Labour Party, enjoying poll leads of around 20 points, described the reports as a 'desperate briefing from a desperate prime minister' to keep up his MPs' morale at Christmas time.

28 December 2023
Rob Murray
Daily Telegraph

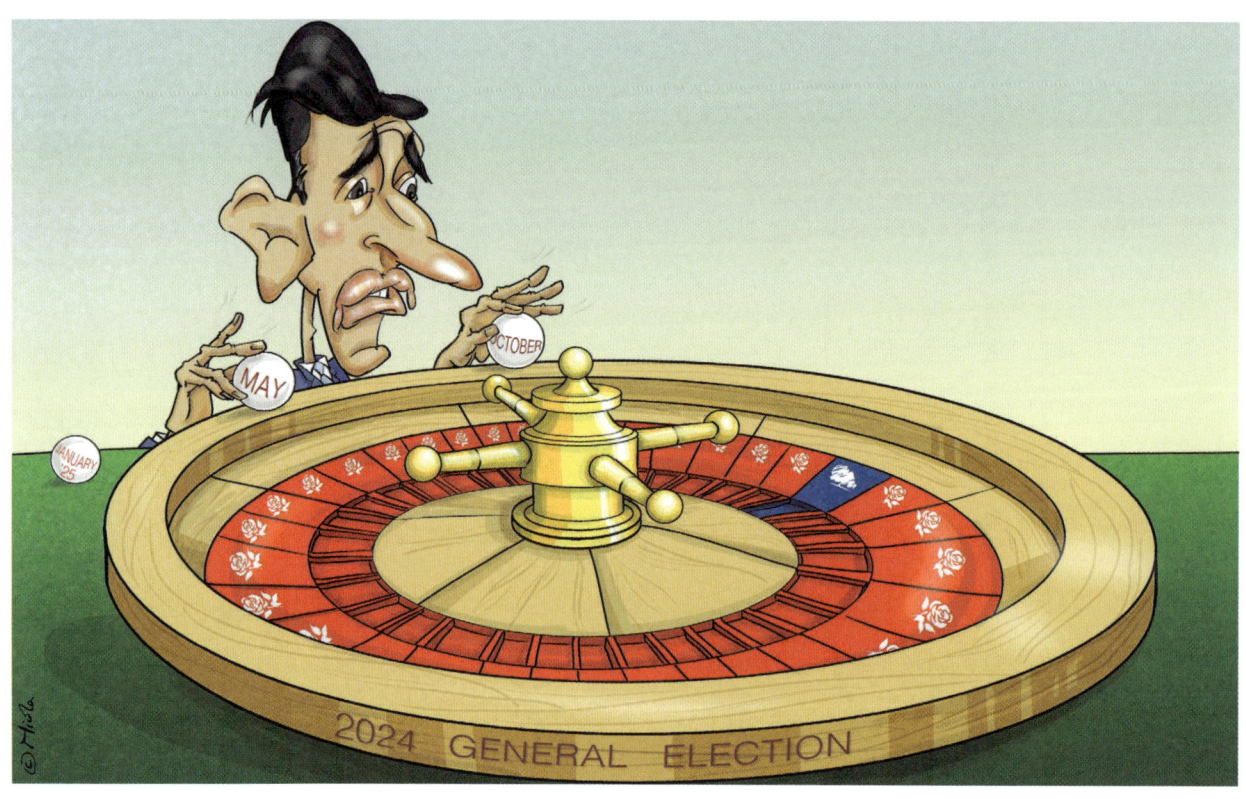

1 January 2024
Nicola Jennings
Guardian

The announcement that the 2024 Budget would be delivered earlier than usual, on 6 March, brought a surge of speculation about a possible general election in May rather than in the autumn. The thinking went that the Budget would be the last big stage on which Chancellor Jeremy Hunt could deliver some good news on tax to cheer Conservative MPs and their potential electors. But with Labour riding high in the polls, the odds still looked to be stacked against a Conservative victory.

On 3 January, junior doctors – represented by the British Medical Association – commenced six days of what the NHS described as the 'the longest consecutive strike action ever taken' in its history. It was part of the junior doctors' fight with the government for a 35 per cent pay rise to make up for what they called a 'real-terms pay cut' over the previous 15 years, caused by inflation. As winter demand on NHS services peaked, there were warnings that hospitals would struggle. Meanwhile, *Doctor Who* was celebrating its 60th anniversary with a series of special episodes aired over Christmas. Ncuti Gatwa was introduced as the fifteenth doctor.

3 January 2024
Graeme Bandeira
Northern Agenda

A row broke out when the government and James Cleverly declared that 112,000 asylum claims had been cleared by the end of 2023 and that the 'the legacy asylum backlog target' had been met, as promised by Rishi Sunak in December 2022. On closer examination, it became apparent that the figures were partly arrived at through expanding the definition of claims deemed to be 'withdrawn' or paused, and by redefining around 4,500 'complex' cases that were mid-process as effectively cleared. Channel 4's FactCheck estimated the total number of outstanding claims to be around 99,000.

3 January 2024
Dave Brown
Independent

Opposition from Republicans in the US Congress continued to stymie the next phase of American military aid for Ukraine's struggle with Russia. Although President Biden wanted Congress to pass a national security bill and release the $61 billion, Republicans – who held a majority in the House of Representatives – were resisting unless Biden agreed to stringent new immigration and asylum measures along the US–Mexican border. Some pro-Trump Republicans went even further, opposing the military aid in principle. Donald Trump had already objected to 'American treasure' being spent on Ukraine.

4 January 2024
Kevin Kallaugher
Economist

6 January 2024
Ben Jennings
i Newspaper

According to an 'unnamed source' in the *Mail on Sunday*, Prince Andrew – who had told the BBC in 2019 that he was unable to sweat – was 'totally tormented' by the imminent release of legal documents. They were from a 2015 civil defamation case brought by Virginia Giuffre against Ghislaine Maxwell, who had been convicted of sex trafficking in association with Jeffrey Epstein. In 2022, Prince Andrew had reportedly paid millions to settle Giuffre's separate historic sexual-assault claims against him, while admitting no liability. Meanwhile, Storm Henk had brought flooding to Wales, York and the West Midlands.

Storm Henk, the UK's eighth winter storm, first hit the UK on 2 January and was one of the season's worst. According to the cartoonist, 'Hundreds of flood warnings remained in place; villages were flooded and commuters faced travel disruption after heavy downpours submerged roads, fields and railways. Keir Starmer said, "Britain can get its future back" once the Tories were voted out; but Sunak's "working assumption" was that he would call the election later in the year since the polls look rather soggy too.' A YouGov poll of 'Westminster voting intentions' placed Labour on 46 per cent and the Conservatives on 25 per cent.

6 January 2024
Andy Davey
Daily Telegraph

" .. to Buckingham Palace ...second class... computer says £114,693."

11 January 2024
Steven Camley
Herald Scotland

The broadcasting on 1–4 January of an ITV television series, *Mr Bates vs The Post Office*, hit a chord with the British public. It dramatised the real-life events of the Post Office Scandal, in which, between 1999 and 2015, more than 700 sub-postmasters and mistresses were wrongly accused of theft and false accounting because their Fujitsu Horizon software was faulty and capable of remote manipulation. Public anger at the miscarriages of justice and the lives ruined now prompted a petition, with 1.2 million signatures, to strip ex-Post Office chief executive Paula Vennells of her CBE honour. On 9 January, she volunteered its return.

The huge upsurge of concern about the Post Office Scandal had ramifications for politicians, including Sir Ed Davey. In 2010–12, as the Coalition government's minister responsible for the Post Office, he had informed Alan Bates, the leading campaigner for the victims, that he did 'not believe a meeting would serve any useful purpose'. While Sir Ed's political adversaries exploited his discomfort, he insisted that the Post Office had lied to him 'on an industrial scale' and spoke of his deep 'regret'. He had often called on politicians of other parties to resign in the wake of their perceived failures. Suddenly, he was under pressure himself.

15 January 2024
Christian Adams
Evening Standard

Donald Trump swept to a record-breaking victory over his rivals in the first Republican primary election, in Iowa, to choose the party's presidential candidate. He won in 98 out of 99 counties, gaining more than 50 per cent of votes and easily beating his strongest challengers, Ron DeSantis (on 21 per cent) and Nikki Haley (19 per cent). It was record-breaking in other ways too: blizzard conditions and plummeting temperatures hit the state during the primary, bringing life-threatening wind chills of nearly minus 35° Centigrade and leading to a low turnout.

17 January 2024
Patrick Blower
Daily Telegraph

On 17 January, Conservative MPs voted through the revised Safety of Rwanda (Asylum and Immigration) Bill. Other parties voted against it, but Sunak also faced discontent from factions dubbed the 'five families' on the Conservative right. They wanted tougher language and explicit rejection of the jurisdiction of international courts: 60 Conservative MPs supported amendments, which failed; and 11, including Suella Braverman and Robert Jenrick, who resigned as immigration minister, voted against the bill. As the cartoonist said, 'Rishi Sunak said his party has "come together" and passed the Rwanda bill . . . The reality is somewhat different: rarely in its history has the party looked so disunited.'

19 January 2024
Andy Davey
Daily Telegraph

With the Rwanda bill passing its third reading in the House of Commons, Rishi Sunak now insisted the 'plan' was working and challenged the House of Lords to approve the legislation swiftly. He also reiterated that he would be prepared, if necessary, to ignore rulings by the European Court of Human Rights that would hinder 'getting flights off the ground'. Given the strength of opposition to the Rwanda scheme in the Lords, Sunak's hopes of smooth travel for a policy that was the offspring of Boris Johnson's premiership (in April 2022) looked distinctly optimistic.

21 January 2024
Chris Riddell
Observer

In the wake of Defence Secretary Grant Shapps describing the UK as 'moving from a post-war to a pre-war world', the departing chief of the general staff called for a 'citizen army' to meet potential threats. General Sir Patrick Sanders spoke warmly of other nations that were 'laying the foundations for national mobilisation' to meet threats from Russia. The classic sitcom *Dad's Army* (1968–77) followed a platoon of the English Home Guard during the Second World War. Its core characters featured the excitable Corporal Jones (catchphrase: 'Don't panic!') and the youthful, scarf-wearing Private Pike, played by the late Ian Lavender, who died on 2 January 2024.

25 January 2024
Christian Adams
Evening Standard

Although Liz Truss's policies as prime minister had quickly made her unpopular with her colleagues, she was behind a new Conservative sub-group called 'Popular Conservatism' ('PopCon'), whose inaugural meeting was now being advertised. Supporters of its libertarian, anti-institutional aims to 'reform Britain's bureaucratic structures' and 'restore democratic accountability' included the Truss-era minister Sir Simon Clarke. In the *Daily Telegraph*, he warned of electoral massacre and demanded that Rishi Sunak resign in favour of a 'prime minister who shares the instincts of the majority' and who could revive Conservative fortunes.

25 January 2024
Dave Brown
Independent

The road ahead looked distinctly troublesome for the Conservatives, as their poll ratings slid further. By contrast, Reform UK was enjoying its highest ratings since the one-time Brexit Party changed its name in 2021. Buoyed by a YouGov poll that put the party on 13 per cent, Reform's leader Richard Tice made, according to the cartoonist, 'occasional threatening remarks about the Tories' chances at the next election, hinting that several MPs may have decamped to Reform UK and that his party could ruin any chance of Rishi Sunak clinging to power. Nigel Farage enjoys the odd taunt as well.'

25 January 2024
Andy Davey
Daily Telegraph

SMOKING BAN – TRUSS INTERVENES!

NOW YOU LISTEN TO ME PRIME MINISTER..!

29 January 2024
Christian Adams
Evening Standard

Liz Truss tried to give her successor some advice by tweeting: 'The Government should abandon its profoundly unconservative plans for the ban on tobacco sales to those born after 1st January 2009. A Conservative government should not be seeking to extend the nanny state.' The plans would, she opined, only please 'those who wish to curtail freedom'. An unimpressed Rishi Sunak told interviewers: 'I don't think there's anything unconservative about caring about our children's health'. The measures, accompanied by a ban on disposable vapes (e-cigarettes), looked certain to achieve healthy bipartisan support in Parliament.

Ever since Boris Johnson negotiated a Brexit agreement, the Democratic Unionist Party (DUP) had objected to the Northern Ireland Protocol as creating an effective trade border in the Irish Sea. The DUP had, therefore, boycotted the power-sharing Northern Irish Assembly and it could not function. On 28 January, Rishi Sunak claimed the new 'Windsor Framework', agreed with the EU, represented a 'decisive breakthrough', bringing smoother trade and guarantees that future laws would not create new trade barriers. DUP leader Sir Jeffrey Donaldson cautiously welcomed the changes, and some notable Brexiteers were impressed; but Johnson and other Brexiteers thought 'divergence' from the EU was being softened.

31 January 2024
Dave Brown
Independent

1 February 2024
Dave Brown
Independent

Scotland's former first minister, Nicola Sturgeon, came under scrutiny as the UK Covid-19 Inquiry moved to Edinburgh. She had told the media in August 2021 that all her communications during the pandemic would be available for examination by a future inquiry – but it transpired that she had already deleted her WhatsApp messages. She defended her actions, saying they were in line with Scottish government policy for WhatsApp messaging and that there was a separate record of anything substantive to do with policy. However, other Scottish ministers had kept their messages, and her political enemies questioned her transparency.

Reviving a familiar tactic, protesting French farmers began blockading major routes into the French capital in what they called a 'siege of Paris'. The ostensible aim was to stop supplies reaching supermarkets. The farmers were angry at taxes on diesel fuel, imminent bans on certain pesticides, and trade agreements that allowed foreign competitors with (they claimed) lower environmental standards to undercut them. The cartoonist commented: 'I always enjoy playing around with difference in scale. To me this is reminiscent of a poster for a disaster or horror film. Something like: *TRACTOR II* – "The farmers are back and they're twice as mad!".'

3 February 2024
Peter Schrank
Economist

DIG FOR VICTORY

LABOUR PLEDGES

Ben Jennings
03.02.2024

3 February 2024
Ben Jennings
i Newspaper

Amid contradictory signals from Labour, some newspapers were reporting that the party was about to abandon its 2021 pledge to invest £28 billion annually in green investment policies, and would not even try to reach that goal mid-term. Rachel Reeves refused to be drawn but reiterated that all Labour spending, if elected to govern, would have to conform first to the party's 'fiscal rules'. A week later, on 8 February, Sir Keir Starmer formally buried the £28 billion promise, saying that it would now be 'irresponsible'. He blamed the decision on higher borrowing costs and the Conservatives 'crashing the economy'.

The Windsor Framework – and a promised £3.3 billion for Northern Ireland – finally enabled the restoration of devolved government in the province's National Assembly at Stormont. Amid much handshaking, Rishi Sunak and the Irish premier Leo Varadkar joined the province's power-sharing leaders: Michelle O'Neill – the first-ever Sinn Fein first minister – and the DUP's Emma Little-Pengelly, deputy first minister. In 1998, as the Good Friday Agreement hung in the balance as a solution to the province's fractured politics, Prime Minister Tony Blair had conjured up the phrase: 'I feel the hand of history upon our shoulder'.

6 February 2024
Ella Baron
Guardian

On 5 February, Buckingham Palace revealed that during King Charles's recent treatment for a prostate condition in the private London Clinic, tests had revealed 'a form of cancer'. The King now returned to London, from Sandringham, to begin 'regular treatments' that would require him to 'postpone public-facing duties'. Messages of support flooded in. Meanwhile, shocking footage of hundreds of people queuing to enrol with an NHS dentist, in the St Pauls area of Bristol, threw into relief the acute shortage of dentists accepting new NHS registrations. A government scheme was offering £20,000 to NHS practices opening in areas of low access.

8 February 2024
Nicola Jennings
Guardian

On 8 February, Vladimir Putin granted a rare interview to a Western journalist, choosing the conservative American commentator Tucker Carlson. Trump-supporting Carlson had previously been highly visible on mainstream US media, hosting *Tucker Carlson Tonight* on Fox News, until he was fired and migrated to social media to launch *Tucker on X*. Following the interview, a seemingly daunted Tucker was widely criticised for allowing the Russian president to dominate the discussion through long and winding monologues, in which Putin pursued dubious historical narratives to justify Russia's invasion of Ukraine.

9 February 2024
Kevin Kallaugher
Economist

At a tense press conference, the 81-year-old President Biden hit back at a Justice Department report alleging that his memory was 'hazy' and 'fuzzy', even when it came to remembering when his son, Beau, had died. Special Counsel Robert Hur was investigating why some secret files, from Biden's time as Obama's vice president, were later found on Biden's private property. Hur concluded that the transgression was not a criminal offence and that, anyway, a jury would regard Biden as 'an elderly man with a poor memory'. Unfortunately, even as Biden rejected the characterisation, he described Egyptian President el-Sisi as the 'president of Mexico'.

9 February 2024
Christian Adams
Evening Standard

Sir Keir Starmer's determination to portray Labour as a party free from antisemitism was put in peril by Azhar Ali, the Labour candidate in the forthcoming Rochdale by-election. At first, Labour defended Ali after he apologised for comments suggesting that Israel had foreknowledge of the Hamas attack of 7 October but used it as a pretext for invading Gaza. But then further comments were revealed, in which Ali referred disparagingly to media figures 'from certain Jewish quarters'. On 12 February, Labour abandoned him and suspended his party membership – though it was too late to replace him on the Rochdale ballot.

13 February 2024
Morten Morland
The Times

17 February 2024
Ben Jennings
i Newspaper

When the Russian prison service reported the unexpected death of the high-profile dissident and anti-corruption campaigner Alexei Navalny, his widow and Western politicians immediately rounded on Putin as being responsible. Just days earlier, Navalny's mother had found her son well, and shortly afterwards he was recorded on video, joking during a court hearing. Navalny had been transferred to a freezing penal colony in Russia's Arctic Circle in 2023, when his sentences for 'extremism' and other alleged offences were extended by 19 years. Now, he joined an expanding crowd of Putin opponents to die in mysterious circumstances.

Mid-February saw two more parliamentary constituencies, Wellingborough and Kingswood, pass from Conservative to Labour with big swings. As the cartoonist explained, 'Veteran pollster John Curtice says the Tories have a mountain to climb. Another ominous feature of the votes is the rise of Richard Tice's Reform UK, which bit into the Tory vote.' In Wellingborough, Reform's Ben Habib won the party's biggest vote-share to date, at 13 per cent. The party's leader, Richard Tice, said the result was 'remarkable' for a 'resurgent party'. Asked if he was concerned about the results, Rishi Sunak said, 'A vote for anyone who isn't the Conservative candidate, whether that's Reform or anyone else, is just a vote to put Keir Starmer in power.'

17 February 2024
Andy Davey
Daily Telegraph

As news of Alexei Navalny's death spread throughout Russia, bands of supporters gathered to place flowers and light candles in his memory – despite the threat of police repression. OVD-Info, a group that monitors dissidents in Russia, estimated that just over 400 people who memorialised Navalny were arrested over that weekend. In describing his approach, the cartoonist said: 'I tried to think of something that showed Putin as a large, menacing presence. Then it occurred to me that this is the wrong way to look at it. He is small and scared, a bulked-up runt who is afraid of flowers and the memory of a dead man.'

19 February 2024
Peter Schrank
The Times

On 19 February, the Department for Education launched a 'crackdown on mobile phones in schools' through new guidance to ban their use 'throughout the school day'. As justification, the government quoted concern from parent surveys and Ofcom figures asserting that 97 per cent of children reaching the age of 12 had phones. However, Gillian Keegan came under fire for overblowing the impact of her department's intervention, given that it was only guidance and between 50 and 70 per cent of schools already enforced phone bans. She fell back on claiming that her new measures included 'break times'.

19 February 2024
Christian Adams
Evening Standard

As foreign secretary under Boris Johnson, Liz Truss had raised eyebrows through her assiduous use of official photographers to portray her as a globe-trotting stateswoman. The press dubbed it 'Instagram diplomacy'. Now, she was on tour promoting her book, *Ten Years to Save the West*. She used a speech at the grassroots Conservative Political Action Conference (CPAC) in Maryland to express her desire to shake up institutions, disrupt 'the woke agenda' and combat the 'deep state'. She also attacked those she regarded as complicit in her downfall as prime minister, including President Biden, the media, the 'corporate world' and the Bank of England.

24 February 2024
Ben Jennings
i Newspaper

As the cartoonist explained, on 21 February 'a parliamentary farce' engulfed the Commons Speaker, Sir Lindsay Hoyle, after he prioritised a Labour motion during what was meant to be an SNP Opposition Day debate on Gaza. Furious SNP and Conservative MPs walked out, accusing Sir Lindsay of helping Sir Keir Starmer avoid a rebellion of Labour MPs supporting the SNP's ceasefire motion. The cartoonist explained how 'The ostensible, albeit arcane, point is the relative merit of "immediate ceasefire" [SNP], "immediate humanitarian ceasefire" [Labour] or "immediate humanitarian pause" [Conservative] – while there is real, acute hunger and desperation across Gaza.' The beleaguered Speaker apologised, pleading concerns about MPs' safety.

26 February 2024
Andy Davey
Daily Telegraph

Lee Anderson remarked on GB News that 'the Islamists' had 'got control of [Sadiq] Khan and they've got control of London and they've got control of Starmer'. He was responding to Suella Braverman's comments in the *Daily Telegraph* that 'the Islamists, the extremists and the antisemites are in charge now'. While Rishi Sunak declared Anderson's remarks 'wrong', he would not call them Islamophobic; but he deprived Anderson of the Conservative whip – only to draw criticism from his right wing for overreacting. Anderson was the most high-profile of those Conservatives who, in 2019, had overturned Labour seats in the so called 'Red Wall' of more northerly English constituencies.

27 February 2024
Patrick Blower
Daily Telegraph

In responding to Lee Anderson's remarks about Islamists controlling London, another Conservative MP found himself in hot water. Paul Scully – the former government minister for London – claimed that there were 'no-go areas' in 'parts of Tower Hamlets' and in Sparkhill, Birmingham, because of people 'abusing' their religion. Politicians of different stripes quickly distanced themselves from him. The Conservative mayor of the West Midlands, Andy Street, lauded Birmingham as 'the most diverse place in Britain' and deplored the 'nonsense slurs' from Westminster. Jess Phillips, a Labour MP in Birmingham, said she was 'expecting an apology for this utter drivel'.

28 February 2024
Christian Adams
Evening Standard

On 28 February, Rishi Sunak told senior police that 'there is a growing consensus that mob rule is replacing democratic rule', intended to 'shut down free debate'. His remarks coincided with an extra £31 million to enhance security for parliamentarians, as tensions over the war in Gaza had resulted in some MPs being subjected to threats and intimidation, even outside their homes. Labour and Amnesty International criticised the 'mob rule' language – language that the police avoided. The *Observer*'s Andrew Rawnsley suggested that the mob rule the prime minister most feared was 'in the ranks of his own party'.

1 March 2024
Peter Brookes
The Times

'Keir Starmer, this is for Gaza,' declaimed George Galloway, the veteran provocateur who pulled off an electoral coup by winning the Rochdale by-election (29 February) easily for the Workers Party of Britain, after Labour disowned its own candidate. Galloway – once a Labour MP himself – warned that Sir Keir would 'pay a high price' in other seats, too, because he had been 'covering for the catastrophe' in Gaza. In the most famous scene from the film chiller *The Shining* (1980), the deranged Jack Torrance (played by Jack Nicholson) axes through a bathroom door as his terrified wife and son try to escape.

4 March 2024
Steve Bright
Sun

CARELESS TALK COSTS ALLIES

you never know **who's** listening!

Blower 5·3·24
Apols to Fougasse

5 March 2024
Patrick Blower
Daily Telegraph

Germany's defence minister claimed that Russia was pursuing a campaign of 'hybrid disinformation' after Russian sources released a transcript of German officers on a video call discussing military aid to Ukraine, including cruise missiles and the possible targeting of Crimea. The German chancellor, Olaf Scholz, called the eavesdropping a 'very serious' breach of security – and German authorities were investigating whether the recording had been altered. The image mimics the 'Careless Talk Costs Lives' poster (1942), produced by cartoonist Fougasse for the British Ministry of Information; in it, Hitler and Goering listen in as two women chat.

Following 27 years as an MP, including 3 years as prime minister, Theresa May announced she would step down at the next general election. Cartoonists had made much of her fondness for sharp dressing and leopard-print heels. In a TV sketch for Queen Elizabeth II's Platinum Jubilee (2022), the much-loved fictional character Paddington Bear, born in Peru, was seen thanking the monarch for her service – and the cartoon evokes an image of the duo by artist Eleanor Tomlinson. However, as home secretary, May had fostered the so-called 'hostile environment' policy in 2012–13, featuring vans emblazoned with the slogan: 'In the UK illegally? Go home or face arrest.'

9 March 2024
Ben Jennings
i Newspaper

10 March 2024
Chris Riddell
Observer

In the Budget (6 March), Jeremy Hunt reduced the rate of National Insurance and took a leaf out of Labour's book on 'non doms' (non-UK domiciled individuals) to make more of their foreign earnings taxable. However, he did not raise income-tax thresholds to reflect inflation, perpetuating the so-called 'fiscal drag'. The BBC's Amol Rajan sparred with Hunt on Radio 4's *Today*: 'They call you the fiscal drag queen of British politics, don't they? And with good reason . . . The net effect of your time in Number 11 is that taxes are still going up.' A non-plussed Hunt replied: 'I don't think I've been called a drag queen before.'

As predicted, Donald Trump (aged 78) and Joe Biden (aged 81) comfortably won their respective parties' nominations to be the US presidential candidate in 2024, promising a repeat of their duel in 2020. Yet, despite the fervour of Trump's MAGA base, large sections of normally Republican and Democratic voters had reservations about their candidates. Meanwhile, on 10 March the 96th Academy Awards were held in Hollywood, where a nominee and winner in several categories was *Poor Things* (2023). In the film, the deceased Bella (played by Emma Stone) has been brought back from the dead, complete with her unborn child's brain.

11 March 2024
Rob Murray
Daily Telegraph

Some newspapers reported the case of Niyak Ghorbani, an Iranian counter-protestor in the middle of a pro-Palestinian demonstration (9 March). Video footage showed him raising a banner reading 'Don't attack the law: Hamas is terrorist', before other marchers grappled with him, trying to tear away his banner. Police quickly intervened 'to prevent,' in their words, 'a breach of the peace'; but they promptly arrested Ghorbani for 'assault' as he shouted 'shame on you'. Following witness claims that the police were heavy-handed and accusations of double standards, a Metropolitan Police spokesperson conceded that Ghorbani was 'de-arrested' after officers reviewed footage of the incident.

11 March 2024
Steve Bright
Sun

Lee Anderson had been suspended from the Conservative Party for his comments about Islamists controlling London. Now, he concluded: 'I cannot be part of an organisation which stifles free speech.' As the cartoonist explained, 'After much teasing of the media, Richard Tice announced that Anderson had defected to Reform UK and would be its first MP.' As for Tice, he claimed that 'Britain is broken. And we all know who broke it.' 'We presume,' noted the cartoonist, 'he was talking about little "Richi" – or maybe the hated liberal elite, or immigrants, or lefties, or the wokerati.'

12 March 2024
Andy Davey
Daily Telegraph

"Do you think this tea towel has been doctored – they're both smiling..."

12 March 2024
Steven Camley
Herald Scotland

Intense speculation swirled around an official Mother's Day photograph showing the Princess of Wales and her smiling children, after five photo agencies withdrew it on the grounds that it had been tampered with. Princess Catherine had disappeared from public view after surgery for an abdominal condition in January 2024, and Kensington Palace's reluctance to explain anomalies in the image, taken by Prince William, fuelled a rumour mill. Then, on 11 March, Catherine broke the silence on social media, explaining that 'like many amateur photographers, I do occasionally experiment with editing' and apologising for 'any confusion'. The unedited image was not released.

The government announced a new definition of 'extremism', encompassing groups aiming to 'destroy the fundamental rights and freedoms of others' or 'undermine . . . the UK's system of liberal parliamentary democracy'. Michael Gove named five groups likely to go on this list of groups banned from government contact or funding, for their alleged Islamist and neo-Nazi aims. There was an immediate backlash, not only from two of the groups, but from across the political and public spectrum, including Conservative Muslim peer Lady Warsi and the Archbishop of Canterbury. Many claimed that there was a lack of consultation and safeguarding (such as an appeals body) and the language used was vague and would encourage division and mistrust.

15 March 2024
Dave Brown
Independent

As new polling put the Conservatives on just 24 per cent, 'Jeremy Hunt promised pensioners he would not let them down – hinting that the pension triple lock would be kept in the election manifesto', as the cartoonist explained. He continued: 'There seemed to be a plot by right-wing Tory MPs to replace Rishi Sunak with Warrior Queen Penny Mordaunt for the general election. Also, little Shapps seemed to have been positioning himself, pointless though such an act would be.' Mordaunt's profile had grown after her sword-bearing role at King Charles's coronation. Hunt soon confirmed the triple lock would stay, future-proofing the state pension against inflation.

17 March 2024
Andy Davey
Daily Telegraph

In one of the year's least surprising events, Vladimir Putin secured victory in Russia's presidential election. His tally of nearly 88 per cent of votes brought him another six years at the country's helm, marking his fifth term as president, and putting him on course to be Russia's longest-serving leader since the days of the tsars. His closest competitor – Communist Party candidate Nikolay Kharitonov – managed just over 4 per cent. With Alexei Navalny dead, Putin's most significant opposition figure inside the country had vanished. The Moscow councillor Boris Nadezhdin – a sceptic about the war in Ukraine – had already been barred from standing.

18 March 2024
Patrick Blower
Daily Telegraph

On 20 March, the government's Safety of Rwanda (Asylum and Immigration) Bill continued to fall foul of the House of Lords, where opposition and crossbench peers pressed for amendments across a range of issues – from consistency with UK and international law to provisions regarding children, and the much-disputed declaration that Rwanda was 'safe'. The parliamentary ping-pong looked set to delay passage of the bill until April 2024 at the earliest. The *Bibby Stockholm* was the controversial barge moored in Portland, Dorset, to house asylum-seekers.

22 March 2024
Ben Jennings
Guardian

In upbeat mood, Rishi Sunak dismissed talk of plots to remove him from Number 10 as merely gossip. Instead, he insisted that 2024 would 'prove to be the year that the economy bounces back'. Sunak was buoyed by the recent news of inflation dropping to 3.4 per cent and signs of growth replacing the shallow recession of late 2023. But for many, such optimism was in short supply. The *Observer* online summed up its cartoon: 'Enter the prime minister on a deflating spacehopper, unaffected by the cost of living crisis.'

24 March 2024
David Simonds
Observer

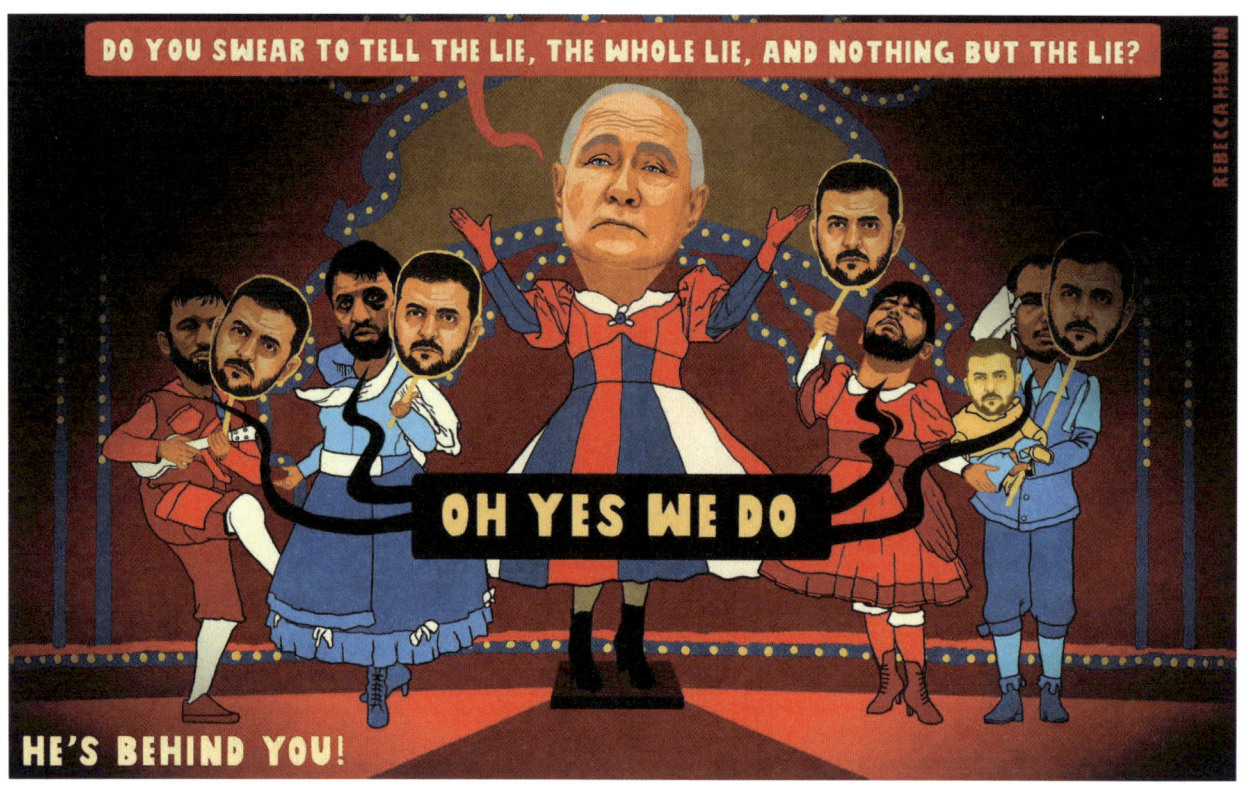

26 March 2024
Rebecca Hendin
Guardian

Despite having no evidence, Vladimir Putin alleged Ukrainian and Western involvement in a mass shooting at the Crocus City entertainment venue in Krasnogorsk, outside Moscow. On 22 March, terrorists killed at least 139 concert-goers and torched the building. An Islamic State affiliate group claimed responsibility and released a video with graphic, violent images. Four Tajik men were soon arrested while trying to flee, supposedly towards the Ukrainian border. Russian state TV later broadcast videos of the suspects saying that their post-attack plan was to 'head towards Kiev', but during a court appearance after their arrest the four had shown signs of torture.

For two months, the position of deputy chairman of the Conservative Party had lain vacant, after Lee Anderson resigned it on 17 January in order to back amendments to the Rwanda bill. Now, his replacement was announced as the pugnacious Jonathan Gullis, another controversial Red Wall MP. He proclaimed: 'I'm ready to take the fight to Sir Keir's hopeless and hapless Labour Party.' The choice seemed to reflect the desire to connect with populist grassroots feelings, though in Anderson's case the strategy had not turned out so well for Rishi Sunak.

29 March 2024
Graeme Bandeira
Northern Agenda

BOAT RACE ...

Ahead of the annual Oxford and Cambridge Boat Race (30 March), the organisers alerted crews to avoid water contact, cover blisters and wear footwear when getting into the boat, after the levels of *E. coli* near Hammersmith Bridge were found to be nearly three times the Environment Agency's limit. This was attributed to Thames Water's release of raw sewage into the river. The warnings put paid to the traditional dunking of the winning cox in the river by his/her crew-mates – and refocused public attention on the controversies surrounding sewage discharge and the dividends paid to water-company investors. The University of Oxford's rowing coach called the pollution a 'national disgrace'.

29 March 2024
Dave Brown
Independent

On 1 April, the Hate Crime and Public Order Act (Scotland) finally came into force, having been voted through in 2021 by the Scottish Parliament. Humza Yousaf, who had nurtured it when he was justice minister, thought it ensured freedom of expression while protecting Scottish citizens from 'threatening or abusive behaviour which is intended to stir up hatred'. But detractors worried that it might stir up culture wars and be abused to pursue vexatious complaints: the *Sun*'s Trevor Kavanagh called it 'a charter for spiteful curtain twitchers'. Meanwhile, police were concerned about the extra workload it might involve.

1 April 2024
Steve Bright
Sun

In Turkey, local election results delivered significant victories to the opposition Cumhuriyet Halk Partisi (Republican People's Party), confirming the trends seen in previous local elections in 2019. Opposition mayors won in a string of important and populous cities – not least Istanbul, with its 16 million people – and with substantial percentage leads. The results were a blow to Turkey's 'strongman' president, Recep Tayyip Erdogan, and his AK Party; they seemed to confirm Erdogan's declining appeal, coming on the heels of his rather slim presidential victory in 2023.

2 April 2024
Patrick Blower
Daily Telegraph

In a round of interviews on BBC and ITV stations in northern England, Rishi Sunak could not resist chuckling when asked about the date of the next general election. 'Why is that funny?' asked Amy Oakden of BBC Radio Tees, 'Why are you laughing about that?' Sunak reiterated his formula that it was his 'working assumption' the election would be in the second half of 2024 and stressed that there was a protocol for announcing election dates. However, his political rivals were quick to make hay, with Labour suggesting: 'Rishi Sunak thinks it's funny that you want a chance to vote for change.'

4 April 2024
Nicola Jennings
Guardian

TIPPING POINT

International outrage followed an airstrike launched by the Israel Defense Forces, which killed seven aid workers in Gaza. The victims, who were almost all foreign volunteers, included three Britons. They had been working for the World Central Kitchen when their convoy was hit. Rishi Sunak and other leaders demanded an independent investigation, while President Biden appeared now to be favouring an immediate ceasefire. There was speculation that a tipping point in world opinion might have been reached, regarding Israel's conduct of the war in Gaza; but it was unclear what weight, if any, international criticism would carry.

4 April 2024
Christian Adams
Evening Standard

Benjamin Netanyahu admitted that the air attack that killed seven aid workers had been an 'unintended strike'. But that mistake threw into relief the dire humanitarian conditions in Gaza and the difficulties of safely providing relief. At the end of March 2024, the International Court of Justice spoke of 'catastrophic living conditions'. At the same time, the body assessing international food crises – the Integrated Food Security Phase Classification – decided that the situation in Gaza had deteriorated so much that 'famine is projected to unfold any time between now and May 2024'.

7 April 2024
Chris Riddell
Observer

On 8 April – the same day that parts of the world witnessed a solar eclipse – Rachel Reeves did a round of media interviews, in which her policies as shadow chancellor risked being overshadowed by questions about Angela Rayner's tax affairs. Following Conservative MP James Daly's complaint to Greater Manchester Police, the force was considering re-examining whether Rayner had fraudulently avoided paying capital gains tax on the 2015 sale of her ex-council home in Stockport. Rayner rejected the allegations, while Reeves told the BBC she was 'absolutely certain' that Rayner was in the clear and that she had 'full faith and trust' in her.

9 April 2024
Christian Adams
Evening Standard

In the United States, crowds gathered to witness the solar eclipse where the temporary darkness would be best experienced. At the same time, Donald Trump's media campaign released a bizarre promotional video. Introduced as 'the most important moment in human history', it intercut footage of assembled crowds with a giant silhouette of Trump's head in profile rising in the sky, like the moon, obliterating the sun rays. 'We will save America and make it great again' was the message. Some commentators quipped that that the concept of Trump plunging the planet into darkness was apt.

9 April 2024
Ben Jennings
Guardian

11 April 2024
Patrick Blower
Daily Telegraph

On 10 April, the NHS published the *Independent Review of Gender Identity Services for Children and Young People*, undertaken by retired paediatrician Dr Hilary Cass. The 'Cass Review', as it was better known, responded to dramatic rises in young people considering gender reassignment and concerns about the advice and treatment offered by the Gender Identity and Development Service (GIDS) at London's Tavistock Centre. As Dr Cass explained, the review found there was 'no good evidence on the long-term outcomes of interventions to manage gender-related distress'. In March 2024, GIDS closed, and NHS England was already restricting the prescription of puberty blockers.

Joe Haines, the friend and press secretary to Harold Wilson, revealed to *The Times* that the Labour prime minister had enjoyed an affair with Janet Hewlett-Davies, a married aide 22 years his junior, during his last term in office (1974–6). Wilson's confidante Lord Donohue, who shared knowledge of the secret, also confirmed long-held suspicions that Wilson had earlier had a brief affair with his influential political secretary, Marcia Williams (Lady Falkender). In Wilson's words as recounted by Lord Donohue, Hewlett-Davies had provided 'a new lease of life'. The Downing Street staircase is adorned with photographs of past prime ministers.

12 April 2024
Peter Brookes
The Times

Kevin Hollinrake, minister for business and trade, asked the Royal Mail to investigate the manufacture and distribution of fake postage stamps. As the cartoonist explained, 'Counterfeit stamps are being sold to unwitting Brits, who are subsequently being stamped themselves with fines. It is alleged that factories in China are mass-producing fake British stamps for export.' A *Daily Telegraph* investigation uncovered four Chinese companies offering to print millions of stamps, complete with barcodes – even though the introduction of barcodes, in 2022, was itself an anti-counterfeit measure. Some politicians thought that the scale of the enterprise suggested Chinese state involvement.

12 April 2024
Andy Davey
Daily Telegraph

It was Sir Keir Starmer's turn to steal his opponents' clothes – and annoy his own left wing – when he promised a 'triple lock' on nuclear defence policy, signalling that Labour would stand firmly behind the UK's nuclear deterrent. To demonstrate his support, Sir Keir visited the shipyard in Barrow-in-Furness where four Dreadnought submarines were to be built, replacing the Vanguard fleet. Promising a 'multi-decade commitment' and attacking the government for reducing the British Army to 'the smallest size since Napoleon', Starmer nevertheless had to field questions about his own past comments rejecting nuclear weapons.

13 April 2024
Ben Jennings
i Newspaper

According to the cartoonist, 'A Tory rebellion was afoot over Rishi Sunak's plan to ban smoking. Liz Truss, Boris Johnson and Suella Braverman prepared to knock over the plans, shouting "nanny-state", "Hail freedom! Fags for all!". It seemed it was one's patriotic duty to take up the weed in the name of liberty. Erm, have they "gone troppo" in the spring sunshine?' In the end, the second reading of the Tobacco and Vapes Bill passed by 383 votes to 67. Braverman and Truss were indeed among those who voted with the 'noes', though Johnson, being an ex-MP, had no vote.

15 April 2024
Andy Davey
Daily Telegraph

The fragile security structures of the Middle East threatened to topple over as Iran attacked Israel with more than 300 drones and missiles, in retaliation for an Israeli strike on Iran's consulate buildings in Damascus (1 April 2024). Helped by international air forces, Israel downed virtually all the Iranian weapons. While Iran declared its retribution over, the question now was: would Israel launch a more devastating reaction? President Biden was quick to tell Benjamin Netanyahu that his country would not join any Israeli attack, and many leaders inveighed against anything that could unleash a wider war. In the end, a single symbolic Israeli missile struck Iran.

16 April 2024
Ben Jennings
i Newspaper

More unwelcome news battered the Conservative Party with revelations concerning Mark Menzies, MP for Fylde in Lancashire and a government trade envoy. *The Times* reported that in December 2023 he had called a local party volunteer in the middle of the night, pleading for £5,000 to pay 'bad people' who, he alleged, had locked him in a flat. Come the morning, his office paid the sum – which had risen to £6,500 – out of party funds. It emerged that an internal party investigation was already under way; but now, Menzies lost the Conservative whip and resigned as trade envoy.

21 April 2024
Chris Riddell
Observer

Despite Sir Keir Starmer's statements on the nuclear deterrent, Conservatives sought to paint Labour as soft on national security because it would not sign up to the government's plans to increase defence spending to 2.5 per cent of GDP. Grant Shapps called Labour's ideas – which included a defence review and building up more incrementally to the 2.5 per cent level – 'delay, disruption and obfuscation'. But his opposite number, John Healey, demanded to know how the Conservative timetable would be funded. Given the polls, the argument was doing little to blunt the Labour advance.

25 April 2024
Dave Brown
Independent

The UK prime minister and the first minister of Scotland might have shared little in terms of political ideology, but both were resembling lame ducks as the threats to their futures multiplied. On 27 April, another disgruntled Conservative MP, Dan Poulter, defected to Labour, and rumours of plots to replace Sunak did not abate. Imminent local elections in England and Wales, on 2 May, looked likely to deliver another drubbing for Conservatives. Meanwhile, having abruptly ended the SNP's pact with the Scottish Greens after falling out over carbon-reduction targets, Humza Yousaf faced no-confidence motions that he had no certainty of winning.

29 April 2024
Nicola Jennings
Guardian

Among government proposals for updating the NHS Constitution were moves to push back against so-called 'gender ideology' and instead bolster a definition of 'sex as biological sex'. The most significant ideas were to make single-sex wards unavailable to trans patients (identifying as a gender different from their biological sex) and enabling patients who need it to request intimate care from an NHS professional of the same sex. The changes announced by Health Secretary Victoria Atkins also hit back against hospital trusts that had deployed gender-neutral language, such as 'chestfeeding', in 'maternal and parental' (maternity) services.

1 May 2024
Patrick Blower
Daily Telegraph

As predicted, local elections on 2 May for 107 English and Welsh councils brought a collapse in support for the Conservatives, not only in the traditional Blue heartlands of southern and rural England but also in the Red Wall Midlands and northern regions. The party lost 474 councillors and 10 councils out of the 17 Conservative-controlled councils up for election. In the councils contested, the Liberal Democrats now had more councillors than the Conservatives. But Sunak insisted that 'disappointing' results had not dented his 'resolve to continue to make progress on our plan'.

6 May 2024
Christian Adams
Evening Standard

Faced with no-confidence votes, on 30 April Humza Yousaf announced he would resign as Scotland's first minister and leader of the SNP, setting in motion a leadership contest. On 2 May, Kate Forbes, who had been Yousaf's rival in the 2023 leadership contest, declared she would not stand – leaving just one contender to be 'crowned': the veteran politician John Swinney. The 60-year-old Swinney had led the SNP in the early 2000s and for several years had been Nicola Sturgeon's deputy first minister. Now, he insisted on his vigour and ambition, declaring 'I am no caretaker. I am no interim leader.'

7 May 2024
Steven Camley
Herald Scotland

10 May 2024
Andy Davey
Daily Telegraph

There was astonishment in the House of Commons when, on 8 May, Natalie Elphicke defected from the Conservatives to Labour. Elphicke, who was MP for Dover, claimed the 'deciding factors have been housing and the safety and security of our borders', but she had previously attacked Sir Keir Starmer as 'Sir Softie' and ridiculed Labour's stance on immigration. In the cartoonist's view, **'**Keir Starmer's decision to allow flag-draped, hard-right Tory nationalist Natalie Elphicke to cross the floor into Labour was met with bewilderment by some of his MPs. It was getting harder by the day to see what Starmer actually stood for.'

Faced with the worsening humanitarian crisis in Gaza, President Biden told CNN's Erin Burnett that the United States would not 'supply the [offensive] weapons and artillery shells' to Israel if Benjamin Netanyahu carried out his plan for a ground operation in the southern city of Rafah. Already, Israeli forces had taken over the Rafah border crossing with Egypt, and already the United States was sending a warning shot by delaying a shipment of 2,000lb bombs. Biden insisted, though, he was 'not walking away from Israel's security', and the United States remained by far Israel's biggest military backer.

10 May 2024
Dave Brown
Independent

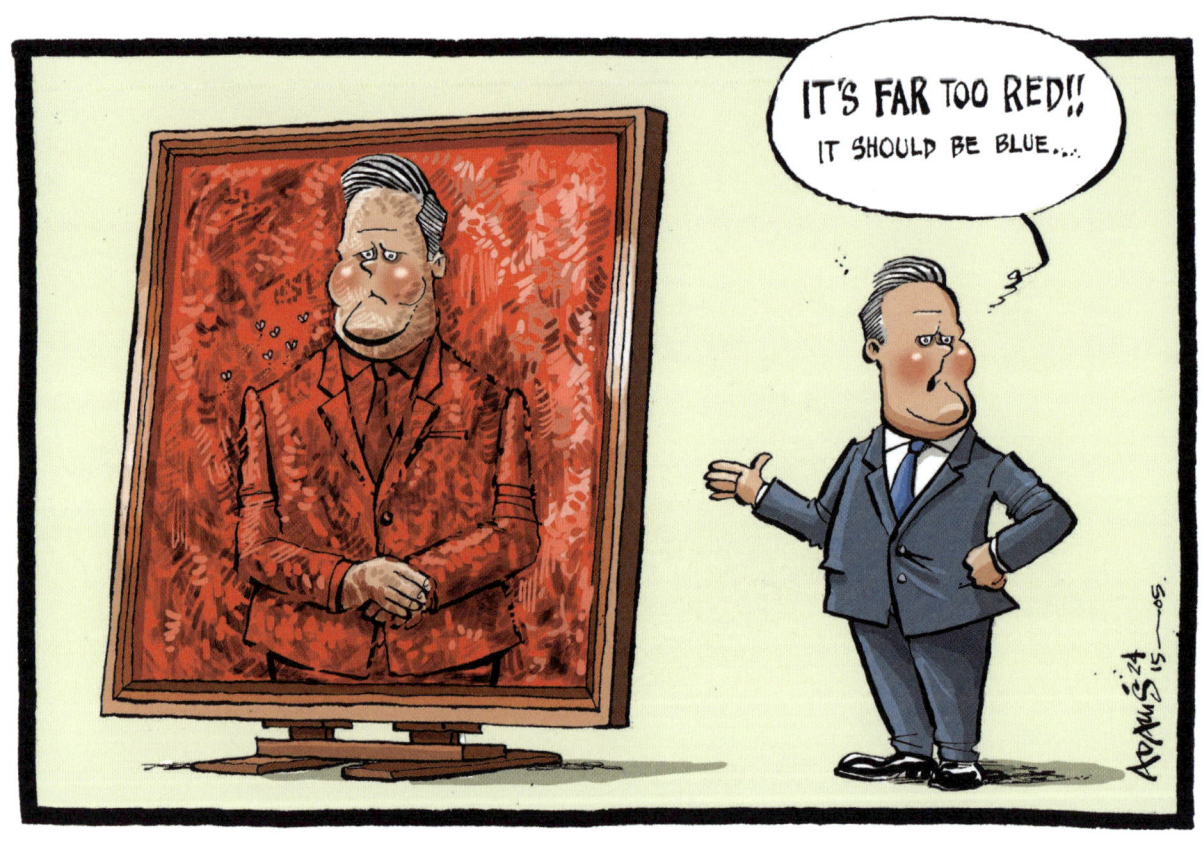

On 14 May, artist Jonathan Yeo's large-scale portrait of Charles III – the first since the coronation – was unveiled by the King and Queen at Buckingham Palace. Commissioned by the Drapers Company, it depicted the monarch wearing the uniform of the Welsh Guards, of which Charles was regimental colonel. In Yeo's words, the 'military regalia subtly fades into the background', creating a sea of red. Yeo painted a butterfly at Charles's shoulder, which, he told the BBC, 'symbolises metamorphosis and rebirth' in the history of art. Sir Keir Starmer's leaning in to traditional Conservative values was seen by some as a metamorphosis too far.

15 May 2024
Christian Adams
Evening Standard

'My first steps for change' is how Sir Keir Starmer billed Labour's six 'pledges' for government, encapsulated on a small card. Less expansive than 2023's 'missions', they spoke of setting up a state green-energy firm (Great British Energy), cutting NHS waiting lists and creating a Border Security Command to interdict people smugglers. They also promised more teachers and action against antisocial behaviour, while ensuring 'economic stability'. The unimpressed Conservative chairman, Richard Holden, thought Sir Keir had 'dumped every pledge that he made during the Labour leadership campaign'. Meanwhile, the eighth film in the *Mission Impossible* series had recommenced production.

17 May 2024
Dave Brown
Independent

18 May 2024
Ben Jennings
Guardian

While remaining tight-lipped about the date of the general election, Rishi Sunak welcomed the Department for Education's draft guidance for schools aimed at stopping discussion of sex, puberty, suicide and other matters below certain age thresholds. The prime minister declared that 'parents rightly expect' that their children 'will not be exposed to disturbing content that is inappropriate for their age'. In addition, the guidance, aimed at primary schools, rejected the teaching of gender identity or raising the concept of a 'spectrum' of genders. Critics worried that children might instead seek information from unreliable sources.

"MY DEEP SORROW IS THAT I THINK INDIVIDUALS, MYSELF INCLUDED, MADE MISTAKES, DIDN'T SEE THINGS, DIDN'T HEAR THINGS." - PAULA VENNELLS

In sometimes tearful testimony, ex-CEO Paula Vennells gave evidence to the public inquiry examining the Post Office Scandal. She was challenged over some past emails and statements suggesting that her overriding priority was to defend the reputation of the Post Office. But Vennells portrayed herself as a senior executive denied fundamental pieces of information about her company's operations, such as the facts that the Horizon IT software contained numerous bugs and that its manufacturer's technicians could manipulate branch accounts remotely. She even denied knowing that the Post Office was carrying out its own prosecutions.

23 May 2024
Ella Baron
Guardian

On 23 May, Rishi Sunak surprised many by announcing a summer general election for 4 July. But the weather accompanying his announcement was anything but summery. Sunak had no umbrella to protect him or his famously tight-fitting suit, which began to gleam as the raindrops flowed down. To add to his discomfort, Sunak's speech was nearly drowned out by the strains of the D:Ream song 'Things Can Only Get Better' – Labour's campaign song in its 1997 landslide – played over speakers by the anti-Brexit campaigner Steve Bray. Inevitably, pundits were quickly labelling the announcement 'Things Can Only Get Wetter'.

24 May 2024
Peter Brookes
The Times

Given the state of the opinion polls, a summer general election was a big risk for Rishi Sunak and the Conservatives. He promised that he would 'fight for every vote'. Sir Keir Starmer welcomed the challenge as 'a moment the country needs', promising to 'turn the page'. As the cartoonist put it, 'Rishi Sunak and Keir Starmer began their general election campaigns in a "hopey-changey" style – it was Sunak's hope (for the polls to change suddenly) versus change (Starmer used the word "change" eight times).' But would their policies address the issues or merely paper over the cracks?

24 May 2024
Andy Davey
Daily Telegraph

28 May 2024
Patrick Blower
Daily Telegraph

No fewer than 75 Conservative MPs – including Dominic Raab, Andrea Leadsom, Kwasi Kwarteng and now Michael Gove – announced that they would not be seeking re-election. Meanwhile, Rishi Sunak and James Cleverly unveiled the Conservatives' policy, if elected, to introduce a form of compulsory national service for 18-year-olds. While the details were vague, Sunak thought that a year spent either in military service or public-service volunteering would inject young people with 'a renewed sense of pride in our country'.

Having conducted what it called a 'carefully considered and proportionate investigation' into Angela Rayner's sale of her ex-council house in 2015, Greater Manchester Police 'concluded that no further police action would be taken'. The force added that matters of 'council tax and personal tax' fell outside its jurisdiction, and that it had passed details of its inquiry to Stockport council and His Majesty's Revenue and Customs: they, too, decided no action was required. Rayner had promised she would resign as Labour's deputy leader if found culpable, but the Conservative-prompted investigation seemed to have done nothing to puncture her career.

30 May 2024
Nicola Jennings
Guardian

In Labour circles, there was confusion about whether it was time for change at the constituency of Hackney North and Stoke Newington, or whether its veteran left-wing MP, Dianne Abbott, would be allowed to stand again. She had only recently regained the Labour whip after a long period in the wilderness following controversy over her newspaper letter suggesting that antisemitism was not racism. While Angela Rayner praised Abbott as a trailblazer and said she saw no reason Abbott could not stand again, Abbott herself was saying she had been barred. Sir Keir Starmer stuck to the line that Labour's National Executive would decide.

31 May 2024
Ben Jennings
Guardian

Both Rishi Sunak and Richard Tice tried to dampen speculation that their parties were discussing pacts, following remarks by Reform's 'honorary president', Nigel Farage. Tice insisted that Farage's comments on the *Sun*'s online show, *Never Mind the Ballots*, were merely 'banter'. As the cartoonist described it, Farage 'sniffed around for some preferment from Rishi Sunak, saying – with characteristic modesty – "I've done them some huge favours over the years . . . I stood aside for Boris to help him win a massive majority [in 2019]. Give me something back." He demanded a "conversation" before the election.' The cartoonist wondered: 'What was Ol' Slimeball up to?'

31 May 2024
Andy Davey
Daily Telegraph

TWINS...

after David Bailey's portrait of the Krays

The Conservatives and Labour tried to tar each other as the party of high taxes if elected to govern. Yet both had committed to not raising income tax or National Insurance rates. Jeremy Hunt now confirmed that a Conservative government would not raise another major source of tax revenue, value-added tax (VAT) on sales, while accusing Labour of planning a VAT hike. Rachel Reeves rejected Hunt's comments, insisting that Labour, likewise, would not raise VAT. In the 1960s, London's notorious gangster twins, Reggie and Ronnie Kray, were just two of the subjects who posed for David Bailey's celebrity photo-portraits.

31 May 2024
Dave Brown
Independent

In May, President Biden announced that Ukraine would be able to use its US-supplied weapons for 'counter-strike' operations into Russia, following the recent Russian offensive against the city of Kharkiv. The decision prompted Russian anger, including from the deputy security chief (and one-time Russian president) Dmitry Medvedev, a man sometimes lampooned as Putin's 'mini-me'. He warned that this 'escalation' meant that Russia could deploy tactical nuclear weapons against 'hostile' countries. In the cartoonist's words, 'Russia is "not bluffing" – little robot Medvedev issues a series of warnings to the West. He is notorious for making frequent and dire threats.'

1 June 2024
Andy Davey
Daily Telegraph

2 June 2024
Steven Camley
Herald Scotland

On 30 May, Donald Trump became the first serving or former US president to receive a criminal conviction. In New York, jurors unanimously found him guilty on 34 charges of 'falsifying business records': fraudulently concealing hush money paid to ex-porn star 'Stormy' Daniels during the 2016 presidential campaign. Throughout the six-week trial, Trump had railed against its legitimacy, and now he pronounced it a 'rigged trial by a conflicted judge who was corrupt'. His sentencing – more likely to be a fine than incarceration – was deferred to July, though the US Constitution allows even an imprisoned felon to run for the presidency.

A key part of Sir Keir Starmer's electoral strategy was to portray himself as a decisive leader. However, Angela Rayner's public support for allowing Diane Abbott to run for her London seat again was widely seen to have pressured Starmer into acquiescence. According to the cartoonist, 'Keir Starmer was dithering over whether Diane Abbott could stand for Labour at the election, amid the widely held belief that Angela Rayner had applied pressure to allow her to do so.' Now, Rayner's comments that she would like to 'get rid of all nuclear deterrents', though multilateralist, were being spun by opponents as another example of Rayner's bold plain-speaking, chipping away at Sir Keir's public commitment to the UK nuclear deterrent.

3 June 2024
Rob Murray
Daily Telegraph

On 2 June, in California, the billionaire Rupert Murdoch married for the fifth time, at the age of 93. His latest bride was the 67-year-old Elena Zhukova, described by the BBC as 'a retired Russian biologist'. Once upon a time, British political leaders craved the support of Murdoch's newspapers – notably the *Sun* – and a close relationship with Murdoch himself. In the modern diversified media landscape, things were different; but Murdoch's favour, his 'emeritus' status notwithstanding, still had potency.

4 June 2024
Ben Jennings
Guardian

On 3 June, Nigel Farage announced that he was replacing Richard Tice as leader of Reform UK for the next 'five years'. Furthermore, he changed his mind about joining the electoral fray, declaring his candidacy for the Essex seat of Clacton. Given his ability to drag media attention to the issues he wanted to stress, his entry into the race threatened further leeching of votes away from the Conservatives. It also promised a constant refrain of complaint about both legal and illegal migration. In the dark folk tale 'The Pied Piper of Hamelin', the vengeful piper's hypnotic music lures children away to destruction.

5 June 2024
Morten Morland
The Times

6 June 2024
Peter Songi
Morning Star

A key part of the Conservatives' electoral strategy was Rishi Sunak's claim that 'independent Treasury officials' had found that Labour's economic plans would drop a £2,000 tax 'bombshell' on British taxpayers. Labour cried 'foul'. However, the Treasury's chief civil servant also declared that the figures 'went beyond' the work of impartial civil servants, and the Office of Statistics Regulation pointed out that the £2,000 figure was spread over four years, not one year. Specifics apart, the characterising of Labour as the party of high taxes was a recurrent theme of Conservative electoral campaigns over the decades.

Rishi Sunak and Keir Starmer sparred over issues such as tax and immigration during their first TV debate ahead of the general election. Sunak sought to present Starmer as an 'unreliable' politician who was 'pursuing power for power's sake', while Starmer accused Sunak of being 'the most liberal prime minister we've ever had on immigration'. As a result of the 'ill-tempered' exchanges between the two leaders, the host of the debate asked them to 'lower your voices'. In the same week, a new season of fan-favourite show *Love Island* aired on ITV.

6 June 2024
Rob Murray
Daily Telegraph

FRENCH EXIT...

8 June 2024
Ben Jennings
i Newspaper

Criticism from all quarters, including centenarian veterans, enveloped Rishi Sunak for cutting short his attendance at events marking the 80th anniversary of the D-Day landings in Normandy (which, in 1944, had begun the liberation of France). 'On reflection, that was a mistake and I apologise,' said Sunak afterwards. Penny Mordaunt described his decision as 'completely wrong' in a TV election debate. It was left to David Cameron, as foreign secretary, to represent the UK in photo-shoots on the former battleground of Omaha Beach alongside President Biden, President Macron and Chancellor Olaf Scholz.

Elections to the European Parliament took place between 6 and 9 June. While parties linked to centrist and centre-left blocs gained a majority of seats, the results also brought success for parties identified with far-right, nationalist and anti-immigration views. In France, the Rassemblement National (National Rally) – formerly the National Front – dominated the poll, with more than 31.4 per cent of votes, dwarfing President Macron's coalition, which managed just 14.6 per cent. Such news might have cheered Nigel Farage, after a protestor threw a banana-flavoured milkshake over him on 4 June, while he campaigned in Clacton.

11 June 2024
Ben Jennings
Guardian

13 June 2024
Dave Brown
Independent

To counteract the image conveyed by Rishi Sunak's multi-million-pound wealth, the prime minister often stressed how hard his doctor and pharmacist parents, both immigrants, had to work to give him opportunities. But in an ITV News interview, he struggled to name the things that he went without when growing up, eventually singling out the paid-for satellite channel, Sky TV. In the *Monty Python* 'Four Yorkshiremen' sketch, four affluent business-men sip brandies and competitively reminisce, in an ever-more surreal and exaggerated manner, about how deprived their childhoods were.

Under pressure during an ITV election debate with Rishi Sunak, Sir Keir Starmer insisted that Labour's manifesto would contain 'no tax surprises', adding that 'there's going to be no need to raise tax on the plans we're setting out'. He said that Labour supported continued freezes on fuel duty, and that raising capital gains tax was 'not a choice we are making'. Sceptics and economic analysts continued to wonder whether all this sunny news hid a gloomier tax forecast, as they tried to place a price tag on Labour's emerging proposals.

13 June 2024
Christian Adams
Evening Standard

17 June 2024
Patrick Blower
Daily Telegraph

On 17 June, Nigel Farage launched Reform UK's manifesto in Wales, calling it a 'contract' with voters. As well as proposing to freeze non-essential immigration, scrap Net Zero targets and extract the UK from the European Convention on Human Rights, Reform also produced an expansive list of spending promises and low-tax pledges, baffling economists. Farage's takeover as leader and his decision to stand had boosted Reform's polling to a level now challenging that of the Conservatives – but adding to an impression that the party was a one-man vehicle. A dismissive Michael Gove characterised Reform as 'a giant ego trip'.

Stonehenge briefly turned orange after two protestors from Just Stop Oil sprayed stones with water-soluble powder paint, on the day before crowds gathered for the summer solstice. The two men wanted to send a message to the next government about ending the extraction of fossil fuels. Rishi Sunak condemned the 'vandalism', while Sir Keir Starmer called the action 'outrageous'. The paint was soon removed by air-blowing techniques, and the solidity of the 5,000-year-old-monument stood in stark contrast to the Conservatives' popularity, as the latest poll predicted as few as 53 Conservative seats in the next Parliament.

20 June 2024
Christian Adams
Evening Standard

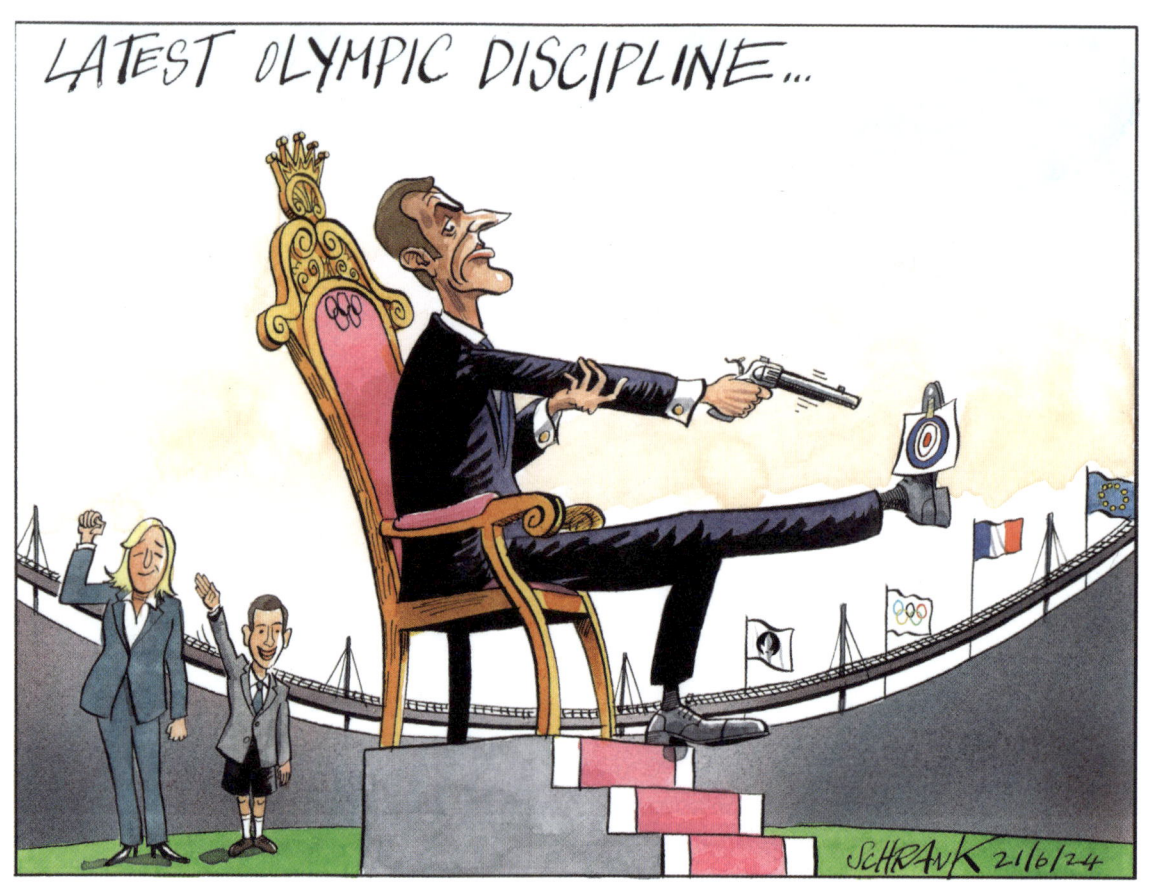

LATEST OLYMPIC DISCIPLINE...

Just weeks before the Paris Olympics, and following the shock gains by the French right in the European elections, President Macron surprised everyone by calling a snap election for the French Parliament – a potentially self-harming gamble. As the cartoonist explained, 'I was pleased to discover that you can translate "to shoot yourself in the foot" into French as *se tirer une balle dans la pied*, and that it is a commonly used expression.' He added: 'I have enjoyed drawing Macron over recent years. His face is easy to caricature, his arrogant charm and imperious ways give us a lot to work with.'

21 June 2024
Peter Schrank
The Times

Mid-election scandal hit the Conservatives, as the Gambling Commission and Conservative Party both opened investigations into whether individuals had used insider knowledge to bet on a July general election date in the days before Rishi Sunak's announcement of it on 22 May. Under scrutiny were Sunak's own parliamentary private secretary, Craig Williams, as well as the party's campaign director, Tony Lee, and his wife Laura Sanders, the candidate for the seat of Bristol North West. By 25 June, the Conservative Party had withdrawn electoral support from both Sanders and Williams.

24 June 2024
Nicola Jennings
Guardian

27 June 2024
Dave Brown
Independent

The long saga of WikiLeaks founder Julian Assange's battle against extradition – to face US espionage charges over releasing US military secrets – finally achieved some resolution. In a complex deal, he was released from London's Belmarsh Prison, flown to the US Mariana Islands, where he pleaded guilty to a single US federal charge of espionage – and was then returned to his native Australia as a free man: it was considered that he had already served his sentence. There were reports that President Biden wanted the issue resolved so that pro-Assange Democrats did not stir up controversy in an election year. The cartoon alludes to the 1994 prison-based film *The Shawshank Redemption*.

Nigel Farage pronounced himself 'dismayed' by the 'appalling' behaviour of Reform UK activists in Clacton, after undercover reporters from Channel 4 filmed them making racist, threatening and homophobic remarks. While one activist described gay people as 'nonces' and called the Pride flag 'degenerate', another canvasser, actor Andrew Parker, called the prime minister a 'fucking Paki' and suggested that army recruits take guns to Dover and use illegal migrants as 'target practice': 'fucking just shoot them', he concluded. A visibly angry Rishi Sunak said Farage had 'questions to answer'.

29 June 2024
Peter Brookes
The Times

30 June 2024
Chris Riddell
Observer

To the alarm of Democrats, and to the delight of pro-Trump Republicans, President Biden lapsed into a faltering, weak-voiced and at times incoherent performance during CNN's election debate between the two rivals. Trump was widely judged to have 'won' this, the first of two planned debates, despite being a convicted felon and making extreme and false claims on matters such as abortion. At one point, Biden mysteriously mumbled that he had 'beaten Medicare' – referring to the federal health-insurance programme for over-65s. A low point was the tussle over who was the better golf player.

According to the final YouGov poll before the general election, Labour was on course for a historic landslide victory. The model predicted that Labour would win 431 seats – the largest number in the party's history – the Conservatives were on course for 102 seats, the Liberal Democrats 72, and the Reform Party for 3 seats including Nigel Farage's seat in Clacton. The poll was far from an outlier, but Keir Starmer warned against complacency, pointing out that 'change will only happen if you vote Labour'. The Wimbledon Championships began on 1 July.

1 July 2024
Patrick Blower
Daily Telegraph

Marine Le Pen's far-right party, National Rally (RN), received the biggest share of the votes in the first round of the French parliamentary elections. RN secured over 33 per cent of the vote following an unusually high turnout. The left-wing New Popular Front coalition secured the second highest percentage of the vote, followed by the Ensemble coalition, which includes President Macron's Renaissance Party. Le Pen cautioned that 'nothing is won, and the second round will determine the outcome', but it seemed as though RN was within reach of being the dominant party. In the Euros football tournament (which commenced on 15 June), Jude Bellingham rescued England by scoring a last-minute injury-time goal to equalise against Slovakia, setting the team up for a dramatic win in extra time.

1 July 2024
Christian Adams
Evening Standard

Boris Johnson made his only campaign appearance on 2 July, giving a surprise speech at a Conservative rally in Chelsea. The former prime minister, whose downfall had been precipitated by the Partygate scandal, said that Labour was on the brink of ushering 'in the most left-wing government since the war with a huge majority'. Johnson used much of his speech to defend his own record on Brexit and the handling of the pandemic and offered no words of praise for Rishi Sunak. Sunak, who had been one of many to resign from the cabinet and force Johnson's resignation in 2023, said in his speech, 'Isn't it great to have our Conservative family united, my friends?'

4 July 2024
Steven Camley
Scottish Herald

The Labour Party won a landslide victory in the general election, winning 412 parliamentary seats and securing the largest majority government in 25 years. The party had increased its share of the national vote by only two per cent but capitalised on the dramatic 20-point drop in support for the Conservative Party; the Tories were down 250 seats to 121 MPs, a historic low. A record 26 senior Conservative MPs lost their seats. Among them was Jacob Rees-Mogg (who had once been chastised for reclining on the front bench of the Commons during a Brexit debate) and former prime minister Liz Truss (who famously lost a competition with a lettuce) who lost her seat in one of the night's biggest electoral swings.

6 July 2024
Ben Jennings
Guardian

Keir Starmer travelled to Washington DC for the Nato summit as prime minister. While there, Starmer had his first face-to-face meeting with US President Joe Biden, at which Biden told reporters that the two countries were 'the best of friends in the world'. The conference was, however, overshadowed by questions about Biden's ability to contest the next presidential election. At the closing press conference, Biden introduced the Ukrainian president, Volodymyr Zelensky, as 'President Putin' and referred to 'Vice-President Trump' when speaking about Kamala Harris, fuelling concerns about his age and abilities.

10 July 2024
Christian Adams
Evening Standard

The new energy secretary, Ed Miliband, ordered a ban on new licences for the exploration of oil, honouring a pledge made in Labour's election manifesto. It was widely believed that Miliband was also considering blocking a handful of outstanding applications approved in 2022. According to the cartoonist, 'Ed got militant and ordered an immediate ban on new drilling in the North Sea in a decision that reversed Rishi Sunak's recent decision, while overruling his own officials. Just Stop Oil, and then some.' Despite reports in the *Daily Telegraph* that Miliband had already ordered a ban on new drilling, a government spokesman clarified that 'existing fields would be managed for the entirety of their lifespan'.

12 July 2024
Andy Davey
Daily Telegraph

On 13 July, former US President Donald Trump narrowly survived an assassination attempt after he was shot while speaking at a rally in Pennsylvania. The shooter, later named as 20-year-old Thomas Matthew Crooks, opened fire from a nearby rooftop: one bullet pierced Trump's ear, while others hit the crowd, killing one man and critically injuring two others. Secret Service agents quickly bundled Trump off stage, but not before he raised a defiant fist to the crowds.

15 July 2024
Steve Bright
Sun

King Charles delivered the Labour government's first King's Speech on 17 July, setting out the new government's priorities. The speech included 39 new bills, including those designed to speed up housebuilding, boost pension pots and bring train operators into public ownership. But the government was widely criticised for not taking the opportunity to scrap the two-child benefit cap. The latest research showed 1.6 million children were missing out on thousands of pounds due to the cap. The charity Action for Children said that the limit was the 'biggest driver of rising child poverty' and the Archbishop of Canterbury, Justin Welby, said the measure is 'neither moral nor necessary'.

18 July 2024
Ella Baron
Guardian

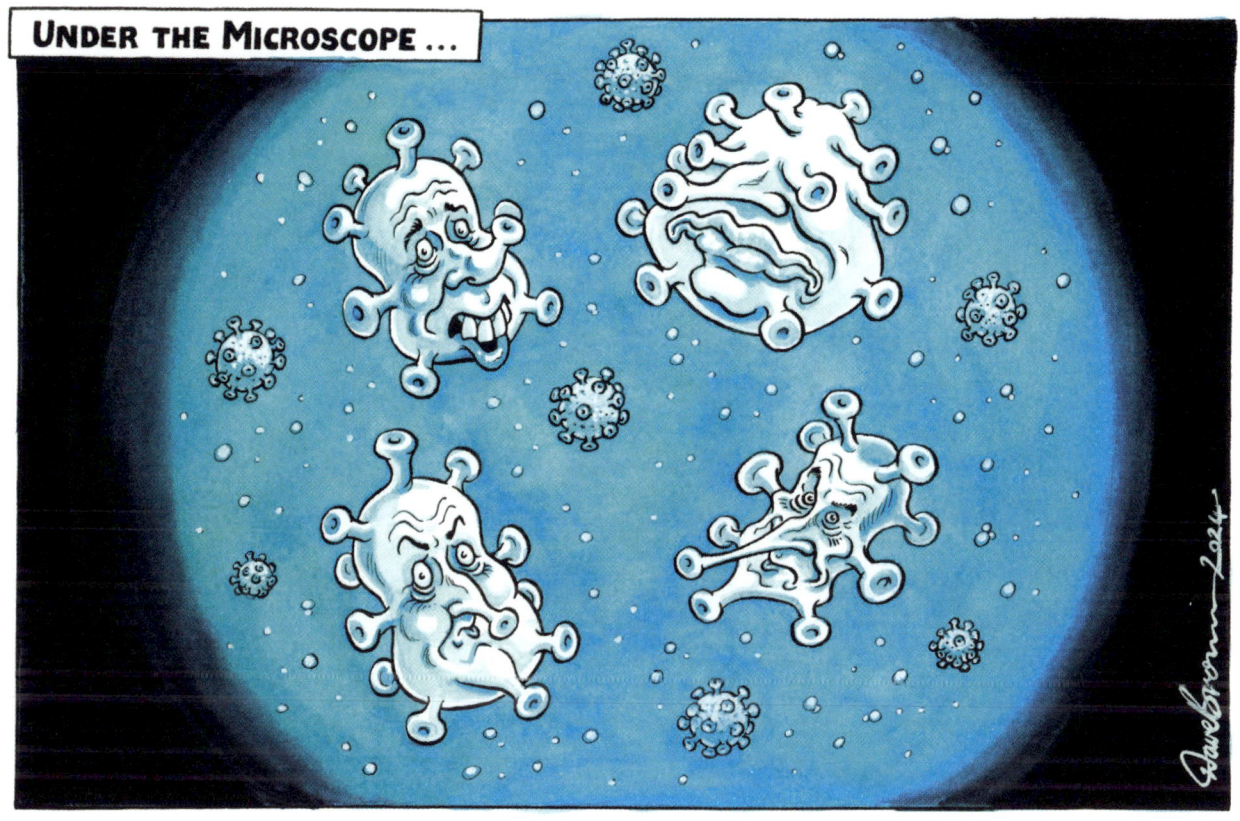

The first report from the UK Covid-19 public inquiry was released revealing 'fatal strategic flaws' in pandemic planning and 'serious errors on the part of the state' in the way it prepared for pandemics. The chair of the inquiry, Baroness Heather Hallett, concluded that lives could have been spared if the UK had responded better, and that the widespread belief that the UK was one of the best-prepared countries in the world was 'dangerously mistaken'. She also called out the former health secretaries Jeremy Hunt and Matt Hancock for their 'lack of adequate leadership' in failing to make better contingency plans.

19 July 2024
Dave Brown
Independent

The prime minister hosted a summit of the European Political Community at Blenheim Palace. Keir Starmer said that he was 'focused on seizing this moment to renew our relationship with Europe' and, after one-to-one talks with President Macron, the two leaders promised to 'strengthen their cooperation on irregular migration' and 'reinvigorate' their defence partnership. As the cartoonist noted, 'Keir Starmer chose Blenheim Palace to reset his relations with Macron and the EU. Diplomacy eh?' Fought in 1704, the Battle of Blenheim saw a decisive victory for the allied English, Dutch and Austrian armies (led by the Duke of Marlborough, Blenheim Palace's owner) against the Franco-Bavarian forces. 'Je viens en paix', translates to 'I come in peace'.

19 July 2024
Andy Davey
Daily Telegraph

The Planning and Infrastructure Bill, one of the new pieces of legislation proposed by the government in the King's Speech, was welcomed by developers as a means to speed up the planning process and deliver new houses and infrastructure. The government announced that local authorities would now have to stick to mandatory housing targets, which would help them keep their promise to build 1.5 million homes over the next five years. Another feature of the bill is that local residents would now only have a say in the style of housing that gets built but not whether it gets built at all, a proposal which angered the so-called NIMBYs (standing for 'not in my back yard').

19 July 2024
Graeme Bandeira
Northern Agenda

On 22 July, President Joe Biden announced that he was quitting his presidential campaign. Following his faltering and forgetful debate performance in June several senior Democrats and party donors had called on Biden to pull out of the race. But, at the beginning of the month, the 81-year-old had insisted that he was 'firmly committed to staying in this race, to running this race to the end, and to beating Donald Trump'. Now he conceded that his withdrawal was 'in the best interest of my party and the country' and backed Vice-President Kamala Harris to succeed him as the Democratic candidate. The cartoonist had to update this cartoon, which originally read 'I'm the only one who can overtake him!', after the last-minute news of the president's withdrawal came through.

22 July 2024
Rob Murray
Daily Telegraph

OVER-USE OF THE WHIP

Keir Starmer suspended seven MPs from the Labour Party after they backed a SNP amendment to end the two-child benefit cap, a policy which Starmer had previously said was unaffordable. Labour won the vote with a majority of 260 but chose to send a message to new MPs by suspending the whip for six months for those who rebelled. The move angered many Labour MPs who had voted with the government. Meanwhile, just days before the start of the Olympic Games, Charlotte Dujardin withdrew from the dressage competition after a video emerged of her 'excessively' whipping a horse. Dujardin was campaigning to become Britain's most decorated female Olympian.

25 July 2024
Nicola Jennings
Guardian

28 July 2024
Chris Riddell
Observer

Chancellor Rachel Reeves said she would give a statement in Parliament about the state of the nation's finances after claiming that an audit of public spending had revealed a 'black hole' in the government's finances. Reeves promised to 'fix the mess we inherited', and a Labour source said the Conservatives 'spent taxpayers' money like no tomorrow because they knew someone else would have to pick up the bill'. Shadow Chancellor Jeremy Hunt said that Labour was 'peddling nonsense' and merely 'laying the ground for tax rises'.

The contest to lead the Conservative Party began in earnest, with six contenders in the race to replace Rishi Sunak: Kemi Badenoch, James Cleverly, Robert Jenrick, Priti Patel, Mel Stride and Tom Tugendhat. According to the cartoonist, 'The problem here was that three of the protagonists, Jenrick, Stride and Tugendhat, are not particularly well known. Drawing a caricature of someone few people will recognise can be a thankless task. Luckily, we are familiar with the others, and they have distinctive characteristics. I particularly enjoy drawing Priti Patel, so my vote would go to her.'

30 July 2024
Peter Schrank
The Times

On 29 July, three young girls were killed in a ferocious stabbing attack in Southport at a dance and yoga event. Eight more children were injured. In the following days, far-right protestors and members of the English Defence League violently clashed with the police after false rumours spread online that the 17-year-old attacker was a recently arrived refugee. Keir Starmer said that the rioters had 'hijacked' a vigil held for the victims of the attack 'with violence and thuggery'. They threw bricks at the local mosque, set cars alight and hurled bottles at the police, seriously injuring several officers.

1 August 2024
Ella Baron
The Times

While sitting down for an interview at the National Association of Black Journalists' convention, Donald Trump falsely claimed that Vice-President Kamala Harris had previously only identified as Asian-American until she recently 'became Black'. 'I didn't know she was Black until a number of years ago when she happened to turn Black,' said Trump. 'So I don't know. Is she Indian? Or is she Black?' At an event later than day, Harris responded that Trump was once again sowing 'divisiveness . . . and disrespect'. Harris has Jamaican and Indian-born parents.

2 August 2024
Ben Jennings
Guardian

Violent riots spread across the country following the murders in Southport and the subsequent disinformation campaign. The Reform UK leader Nigel Farage was accused of helping to incite far-right violence after he posted a video on social media questioning why the police were not treating the attack as terror-related and asking if 'the truth is being withheld from us'. He later took to social media to confirm that he did not support the riots but that the violence was 'nothing [compared] to what could happen'. Steve Rotheram, the mayor of Liverpool, said that Farage was 'giving [the protestors] some legitimacy to go out and perpetrate some of these acts'.

2 August 2024
Dave Brown
Independent

Three Americans, including reporter Evan Gershkovich and US Marine Paul Whelan, stepped back onto US soil on 1 August after being imprisoned in Russia. They were met by President Biden, Vice-President Harris and their families, after the Biden administration negotiated a prisoner swap involving seven countries and 24 prisoners – the largest such deal since the Cold War. Donald Trump, who had previously claimed that he was the only one who could secure the prisoners' release, now took to social media to call the negotiators an 'embarrassment'. 'Are we releasing murderers, killers, or thugs?' asked Trump. 'Just curious because we never make good deals, at anything, but especially hostage swaps.'

4 August 2024
Ella Baron
The Times

BILLIONS STAND BEHIND ME!

The British government criticised Elon Musk after the billionaire posted on X, the social media platform he owns, that 'civil war is inevitable' underneath a video of violent riots in Liverpool. A government spokesman responded that there was 'no justification for comments like that'. But Musk continued to criticise Keir Starmer online, referring to him as 'two-tier Keir' in reference to conspiracy theories peddled by Nigel Farage and far-right activist Tommy Robinson that the British police were treating white, far-right protestors more harshly because of their race and political views. Musk also shared a fake article, made to look like it was published by the *Daily Telegraph*, falsely claiming that protestors were being sent to 'emergency detainment camps' in the Falklands.

8 August 2024
Dave Brown
Independent

Anti-racism demonstrations took place in several cities across England on 7 August in response to plans for more far-right anti-immigration riots. Around 25,000 people gathered in Bristol, London, Birmingham, Liverpool, Brighton and other cities, holding 'refugees welcome' and 'unite against hate' signs, after police warned that up to 100 more rallies were being planned by the far right. In Liverpool, over 2,000 people formed a human shield around St Anne's Church which hosts an immigration centre and was thought to be on the rioter's 'hit list'.

8 August 2024
Christian Adams
Evening Standard

Conservative leadership candidate Robert Jenrick was criticised after he said that any protestors shouting 'Allahu Akbar' should be 'immediately arrested'. Speaking about claims that far-right protestors were being treated more harshly than protestors at last year's pro-Palestinian demonstrations, Jenrick said that he 'thought it was quite wrong that somebody could shout Allahu Akbar on the streets of London and not be immediately arrested . . . That attitude is wrong and I'll always call out the police for it.' Labour MP Naz Shah responded, 'This is complete ignorance and textbook Islamophobia . . . It literally equates every Muslim in the world with extremism.'

9 August 2024
Dave Brown
Independent

A state of emergency was declared in the Russian region of Kursk, after Ukrainian troops launched a cross-border attack on 6 August. Over the next few days Ukrainian forces advanced further into Russia, constituting the deepest foreign advance into Russian territory since the end of the Second World War. According to the cartoonist, 'You never know where an idea might come from. Here it was simple: I wanted to draw Putin sucking his thumb. That would be in line with my theory that most despots overcompensate for their feelings of inadequacy. A twist on the old "reds under the bed" scenario gave me the setting.'

10 August 2024
Peter Schrank
The Times

The Democratic Party caught the attention of voters and the media by consistently criticising their Republican opponents as 'weird'. The trend was attributed to Tim Walz, Kamala Harris's running mate, who said in a speech that 'These guys are creepy and yes, just weird as hell.' Trump retorted that 'They're the weird ones. Nobody's ever called me weird. I'm a lot of things but weird I'm not.' Meanwhile, Trump was mocked after footage posted to X appeared to show him waving to empty tarmac while stepping off a plane in Wisconsin to create the impression that he was greeting a large crowd. He had repeatedly accused his Democratic rivals of using artificial intelligence to generate fake images of larger audiences at their rallies.

17 August 2024
Morten Morland
The Times

Donald Trump took part in a rambling two-hour conversation with Elon Musk on X. During the unorthodox interview Trump praised Vladimir Putin and North Korean leader Kim Jong Un as being 'at the top of their game' and he simultaneously insulted Kamala Harris as 'a radical left lunatic' and praised her as being like 'the most beautiful actress ever to live'. He also alleged that he attempted to discourage Putin from invading Ukraine while president: 'I said: "Don't do it. You can't do it, Vladimir" . . . I told him what I'd do, and he said, "No way," and I said, "Way!" ' The latest polls showed Harris leading Trump by five percentage points.

18 August 2024
Chris Riddell
Observer

The transport union ASLEF announced that its members working for the train company LNER would strike for 22 days in a dispute over management practices. The union emphasised that this issue was separate from the years-long stand-off with 16 train operators over pay. The new Labour government had recently offered transport unions a revised deal which would result in pay rises of nearly 15 per cent over three years. It had also offered junior doctors a 22 per cent pay increase to end NHS strikes. According to the *Daily Telegraph*, the offers 'sparked fears that [the Chancellor] would have to put up taxes in her first Budget to cover the spiralling cost of the government wage bill'.

19 August 2024
Patrick Blower
Daily Telegraph

ANOINTED

ANNOYED

ROB MURRAY
24·08·24

Kamala Harris promised to offer a 'new way forward' for America as she officially accepted her party's nomination for president at the Democratic convention in Chicago. The main message of the convention was 'joy', in contrast to what Secretary of Transportation Pete Buttigieg referred to as the Republican candidates' 'darkness'. Harris's opponent, Donald Trump, responded by posting 58 times on Truth Social during Harris's acceptance speech, accusing her of 'gaslighting', and calling her 'Comrade'. Immediately afterwards, he called Fox News to deliver an on-air tirade against Harris's speech that was eventually cut off by the network's hosts.

24 August 2024
Rob Murray
Daily Telegraph

Keir Starmer warned that as a result of the 'rot' left behind by the Conservatives, his government was preparing to make some 'unpopular decisions'. The prime minister described his government's inheritance as no more than 'rubble and ruin' and said that 'we have to take action and do things differently. Part of that is being honest with people about the choices we face. And how tough this will be.' MPs were due back from the summer recess, and it was widely expected that the government was preparing to announce tax increases and cuts to public services.

26 August 2024
Rebecca Hendin
Guardian

NASA announced that two astronauts stranded on the International Space Station would not return to Earth until February 2025. Pilot Sunita Williams and Commander Barry Wilmore blasted off on 5 June and were meant to stay in orbit for only eight days. However, problems with their spacecraft's propulsion system meant the astronauts' return to Earth was repeatedly delayed. According to the cartoonist, 'I'm not completely happy with this caricature of Keir Starmer. He started regularly wearing glasses around the beginning of the election campaign. Perhaps someone told him they made him look more prime-ministerial. The glasses make him more difficult to draw by obscuring his very deep-set, somewhat anxious eyes and covering the bridge of his nose.'

26 August 2024
Peter Schrank
The Times

The prime minister promised to 'turn a corner on Brexit' and rebuild relationships with EU member states in advance of his trips to Berlin and Paris to meet with EU leaders. Starmer said the international visits were part of wider efforts to 'reset our relationship with Europe and strive for genuine, ambitious partnerships' as well as heal 'broken relationships left behind by the previous government'. Starmer insisted, however, that he was not seeking to reverse Brexit, nor was he prepared to join any youth mobility schemes (such as the one signed between France and Germany in 2019) as part of his renewed relationship with the EU.

28 August 2024
Christian Adams
Evening Standard

ONE FOOT IN ..?

Donald Trump was criticised by veterans for turning an anniversary event at Arlington National Cemetery into a campaign video. The video posted to TikTok shows Trump walking past the graves of servicemen killed in Afghanistan in 2021, while the voiceover blames President Biden and Kamala Harris for American deaths in the conflict. Trump posed for photos at the site which show him smiling and making a thumbs-up sign. Furthermore, two of his campaign staffers were accused of verbally abusing and pushing a cemetery official who tried to stop them filming. In 2019, Trump's former attorney, Michael Cohen, claimed that the former president told him he had avoided serving in the Vietnam War by convincing a doctor to make a fake diagnosis of bone-spur injuries.

31 August 2024
Dave Brown
Independent

31 August 2024
Ben Jennings
i Newspaper

Keir Starmer revealed that his government was considering an outdoor smoking ban that would apply to areas such as pub gardens and outdoor restaurants. This would be in addition to existing proposals to gradually make smoking illegal year by year. Minister of State for Skills Jacqui Smith told *Sky News* that the ban would help people to 'reduce their smoking and to cut the 80,000 people who die every year from smoking-related diseases'. In other news, after a 15-year split, brothers Noel and Liam Gallagher announced that their band, Oasis, would reform for a reunion tour. The announcement on the band's social media accounts read, 'This is it, this is happening'.